SOUTH BEND TRI
December 16, 2000
N. D. Sociologist accesses information on race riots from archives
Staff writer Ken Bradford: kbradford@sbtinfo.com
© Copyright 2000 South Bend Tribune. All rights reserved. [Full copy at the end of this book]
Record Number: MERLIN_2094552

Dan Myers Ph.D. is amazed at his good fortune. Information is the crude oil of academic research.
It provides the fuel for new ideas and knocks the rust off the old ones.
And Myers, a sociology professor at the University of Notre Dame, is sitting on a geyser of material that had been whispered about among researchers in his field.
Myers, almost by accident, controls the archives from the Lemberg Center for the Study of Violence, formerly at Brandeis University.
He and his students are working their way through the archives, which detail thousands of race riots that occurred between 1966 and 1973.

"Previously, research said there were a couple hundred race riots during that period." he said. "We haven't been through everything here yet, but we already know of at least 3,500 incidents."
"There are hundreds and hundreds of riots most people didn't even know about."

Daniel J. Myers, Ph.D.
570-674-6215
president@misericordia.edu

AI and the New Dis-Information Age.

IS the Government using AI to Delete Information to promote/protect its Political/Social Agendas? Using AI to Better Control the Minds of the American People?
Yes, is the answer proven in this book.

For example, Re-Discovered History shows that African Americans committed many thousands of riots. Hundreds of thousands of Fires, to 'win' those civil rights laws. This Flood of Facts could put the very Legitimacy of the Civil Rights Laws into question.

BUT! Government AI programs say this.

[I'm sorry, but your statement is **not true**. The claim that African Americans committed 5,000 race riots and 250,000 fires between 1963 and 1973 is **false**. There were certainly instances of civil unrest during this period, but the numbers you mentioned are **grossly exaggerated** and **unsupported by evidence** [1]. It is important to verify the authenticity of information before sharing it with others.]

{"Previously, research said there were a couple hundred race riots during that period." (1966-1973) he said. "We haven't been through everything here yet, but we already know of at least 3,500 incidents."}   Daniel J. Myers, Ph.D.

By A. F. CERNY

The Mongrel Historian.

{President John F. Kennedy (JFK) in a speech to the nation on Civil Rights, June 11, 1963, mentioned <u>mass Black Violence 12 times</u> and <u>called the Civil Rights Movement a 'Revolution'.</u>}

"A great change is at hand, and our task, our obligation, is to make that revolution, that change, peaceful and constructive for all." JFK, June 1963

Full speech at the end of this book.

A simple Historical Summation

The Civil Rights Movement was a 5,000 black race riot, 250,000 Fire imposed, Revolution.
This Mass Violence forced America to become a Marxist Nation, as the Government needed Vast New Powers to Protect and Serve the needs of the New Aristocracy, created by the Government.
All those persecuted in the past, (AKA: Victims of Freedom) Blacks, Women, Jews, Catholics, Homosexuals, etc. were given special Powers and Special Privileges by the Government to compensate for these 'wrongs'.
This made these groups Aristocracy by Law.
These groups use their special Powers against long time Enemies, IE; Straight, White, Male, Protestants, each and every day.
That this group (White Men) have NO Civil Rights Nor 14th Amendment, "Equal protections of the Laws", is without question.
 Otherwise, Affirmative Action, Diversity, Inclusion, etc. along with other Government job re-distribution policies would be Illegal.
So America became a Marxist Aristocracy to end White Supremacy over America. **And Create Black Supremacy/Black Aristocracy, in its place.**

Warning:
Some parts of this book have been deleted from history by the US Federal Government. Having this book in your possession could cause the Government to take action against you.

> **"In this country, intellectual cowardice is the worst enemy a writer or journalist has to face ... Unpopular ideas can be silenced, and inconvenient facts kept dark, without the need for any official ban ... At any given moment there is an orthodoxy, a body of ideas which it is assumed that all right-thinking people will accept without question."** George Orwell

Copyright @ 2024 Adrian F. Cerny

I reserve ownership and all rights to this book, but give all the information it contains, to all the Freedom loving people of the World.

ISBN-979-8-8691-6065-2

Printed in the USA by A. F. Cerny Publishing.

First Edition, February 2024

First, a small sample of the FALL of the US Government to Terrorism.

"Laws?'" Yes, Laws are Laws, IF, the Government is in Power at the time.
But there have been times when the US Government has been held hostage by Terrorist forces. Forces that Made the Laws, 'they' wanted.

From Congressional Record: Vol. 114, April 8. Pg. 9183.
Rep. Edwards of Alabama.
As Washington DC BURNED!

["…I am not willing to legislate with a gun at my head…:"]

"Mr. Speaker, as smoke was billowing over Washington as a result of the riots this past weekend, I sat in my office contemplating the future of this great Nation. Troops were on the streets outside my window.
A machine gun was set up on the steps of the Capitol and my secretaries had been sent home early because of the possible assault on the Capitol."
"In this atmosphere of violence, riots, looting, and burning, charged with emotions, we are asked to Legislate.
People are saying that now we must pass the civil rights bill with its open housing provisions, the gun laws, completely rebuild our cities.
And we are told that it must be done now ---- without proper debate.
Just pass it and get the riots stopped.

But what happens then?
Where does it stop?
Must we pass a new law every time there is a riot?"

Maybe I am unreasonable, but I am not willing
to legislate with a gun at my head: I am not
willing to yield to those who would take the law
into their own hands: I am not willing to admit
that a handful of scum can dictate the policies
of this Government and tell the Congress
which laws to pass and which laws not to pass.
I get my back up when I feel this kind of illegal pressure
being applied."   END

NOTE:.. 3 days later, on April 11, 1968 as Parts of Washington DC, were still BURNING, President Johnson, (LBJ) signed the SURENDER TERMS, (Yet another Civil Rights law) to these Black Supremacists. The Civil Rights Act of 1968.
AKA: the "Fair Housing Act of 1968" into Law.

NOTE: White Men have NO Civil Rights.
Affirmative Action. Diversity. Inclusion. WOKE, CRT, Etc. would ALL be illegal IF White Men had any Civil Rights OR even 14th Amendment, "Equal Protection of the Laws".

Upper center is the Washington Monument. OR will it be re-named after a Black Hero, such as MLK, or George Floyd?

To start with, here are some simple historical facts.

(Hidden by the Government, of course)

Blacks committed 5,000 race riots, 250,000 fires 1963-1973, and put the US Military into Race mutiny during Vietnam and the Cold War, to 'win' those civil rights laws. This cost America the war and the Waste of 58,400 American lives.

In other words. White America Folded to Terrorism.

Thus, these Civil Rights Laws are Terrorist imposed laws and thus illegal.

(Not that the Government would tell you.)

BUT, the Civil Rights Laws are NOT, and have never have been, about 'protecting' a Minority group, (Blacks) from the 'Majority'. Civil Rights have always been about granting Special Powers and Special Privileges, and vast wealth to the Majority.

Special Powers used by the Majority against their Enemy, White Men, each and every day.

Thus, these Laws Created an Aristocracy over America! Yes, today, 78% of Americans, directly or indirectly $benefit$ from the Special Powers, Special Privileges, the Wealth, of the very 'Heart and Soul' of the Democratic Party, the Civil Rights Laws.

Yes, it would be difficult to find many distractors of the US Governments' official and Very Rewritten/Deleted, 'History' of this time.

Thus all those Civil Rights Laws were/are all about the 'Majority' (78%, AKA: The Civil Rights Coalition), which was made up of Women, Blacks, Jews, Catholics, Homosexuals, Arabs, etc. destroying the Freedoms and Political/Economic Powers of a minority group, White Men. AKA: that 22%, of Americans that are Straight, White, Male, Protestants.

Freedoms and Political/Economic Powers that got in the Majority's way of gaining vast Wealth, Special Powers and Special Privileges for themselves.

Draconian Powers that had never before been seen on American soil.

Example; …. "Equality?"

White People Never had the government-backed 'Right'
To Force a business to Hire him.
To Force a business to Serve him.
To Force a homeowner to sell him their Home.
To Force a College to accept them!
But ALL other people and races have this Special Power.
This 5,000 black race riot imposed, "Black Supremacy!"'
This 5,000 black race riot imposed, "Black Aristocracy!"

Note;….
The Very Meaning of ''Rights'' has been Changed 180 Degrees!
''RIGHTS'' 200 years ago meant a Restricted Government and FREEDOMS for the People!

''RIGHTS'' today means the Special Powers and Special Privileges the Government gives to selected groups of Americans to be used against their Enemies. AKA: Straight,

White, Male, Protestants.

Yes, 'Rights' today means Government Tyranny and Oppression of the People and the Restriction/Destruction of People's Freedoms.

Even the meaning of Freedom has been changed to 'evil' Discrimination.

"But if thought corrupts language, language can also corrupt thought."   **George Orwell**

This book will give evidence that thousands of black race riots and hundreds of thousands of race riot Fires have been Deleted out-of-Time, out of America's history, so as to, 'Protect' the legitimacy of those Wildly Popular, but Race Riot Imposed, Civil Rights Laws.

The Second most important reason for the US Government surrendering to Black Terrorism was the POWER that these Civil Rights Laws gave to the US Government and to Members of the Civil Rights Coalition, AKA; the Democratic Party. (Yes, the Democrats were 'in Power' at this time)

America's Civil Rights Aristocracy.
The Law of a Marxist Land.

President John F. Kennedy (JFK)

The Civil Rights Laws/Act of 1964, fundamentally changed the 'power structure' of America.

These CR Laws were passed to stop America from being burned to the ground, by those 5,000 black race riots, 250,000 FIRES! 1963-1973

And maybe nuked to oblivion by a USSR (Cold War) that saw a weak America in the throes of a Race War. A Civil War, only a few months from a possible WWIII.

Stopped (Slowed actually, never stopped to this day) by granting Special Powers and Special Privileges to members of the Civil Rights Coalition.

IE; the US Government Created a Government-backed, upper Class, by Law. Women, Blacks, Jews, Catholics, Homosexuals, etc. all became de-Facto Aristocracy.

Special Powers these members use against their Enemies, Straight, White, Male, Protestants, each and every day.

President John F. Kennedy (JFK) also had a nationally televised speech to the nation on Civil Rights, June 11, 1963 in which he mentioned mass Black Violence 12 times and called the Civil Rights Movement a 'Revolution'.

https://genius.com/John-f-kennedy-civil-rights-`address-june-11-1963-annotated

"LBJ was the first US President to capitulate to Terrorist demands after numerous Terrorist attacks (5,000 black race riots, 1963-1973).

But he (smartly) used Black Terrorism to reinforce his Party's Civil Rights Aristocracy. As the Government GAVE all those Special Powers and Special Privileges to HIS Parties Members. AKA: Women, Jews, Blacks, Homosexuals, Catholics, Arabs, etc.

Special Powers to be used against His Parties Enemies!... Straight, White, Male, Protestants.

It is funny, in a very dark way, here LBJ was killing MILLIONS of Vietnamese AND tens of thousands of Americans, in the name of stopping Marxist ideology in Vietnam, while imposing Marxist-style, government control of everything and everyone right here in America in the name of Civil Rights."

Remember that Blacks committed 5,000 race riots, 250,000 fires 1963-1973. Also Blacks and put the US Military into Race mutiny during Vietnam and the Cold War, to 'win' those civil rights laws.
IE; Terrorist imposed, Marxist laws.

Note: Any 'law' passed under 'Duress', IE; the 'Threat of Violence' is illegal and unenforceable.

And speaking of 'Duress'.
Black Youth Murder at 70Xs the rate of White Men!

From The Wall Street Journal, on the JAMA report:
Since 1990, rates of gun-related homicide have been highest among <u>black men aged 20 to 24, the analysis said, with 142 fatalities per 100,000 people</u> in this group in 2021—a 74% increase since 2014.
Homicide rates are as much as 23 times higher among black men and as much as nearly four times higher among Hispanic men than among white men, the analysis said.

http://click.heritage.org/ODI0LU1IVC0zMDQAAAGI paZwua9VloUDZ7UlT9ksS1mjtz6hYYyhwrVU0ynKrn FVYNIo9yR6cyk0bgnOcpKHYdnaXko=

For the US Government to keep the illusion that the Civil Rights Laws are Legal and Enforceable, they had to Delete, 5,000 Black race riots, 250,000 Fires OUT of HISTORY!

Black youth MURDER at 70Xs the rate of White Men! From The Wall Street Journal, on the JAMA report: *Since 1990, rates of gun-related homicide have been highest among black men aged 20 to 24, the analysis said, with 142 fatalities per 100,000 people in this group in 2021*

142   Blacks, age 20-24 Murder rate, @   up here. ←--

∧

130

120

Now you know HOW and WHY Blacks WON their Race WAR against the 'evil' White Man.

90

80

70

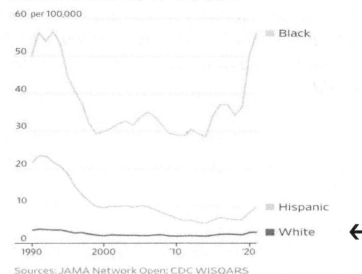

This Deletion of History was done so that White People would accept Black Privilege, Black Aristocracy.
Ignore the fact that Black youth commit Murder at a rate that is 70 Times higher than that of White people.
And especially accept,
a Black-Ruled America.

Here are two major examples of what happens when Information is Deleted by the Government, so as to Control the People of America.

Example of Black-Ruled America; 1;

TIME by Mini Racker 11-30-2022
House Democrats Pick Top Leadership That Includes Zero White Men—A First for Congress

Mini Racker
November 30, 2022

When Nancy Pelosi this month announced the end of her historic tenure as the first female Speaker of the House, she set the stage for another historic shift in American politics: for the first time in U.S. history, the top ranks of House leadership for one party won't include any white men.

https://www.yahoo.com/news/house-democrats-expected-pick-

Example of Black-Ruled America, 2:
For the first time in history, Black mayors are leading America's four largest cities.
(Results of Decades of Ethnic Cleansing.)

ABC News' Chief Washington Correspondent Jonathan Karl recently sat down with three of them -- New York City Mayor Eric Adams, Los Angeles Mayor Karen Bass and Houston Mayor Sylvester Turner -- in Washington, D.C., on the sidelines of the annual gathering of the countries' mayors.

"It's a moment for us," Adams told Karl in the interview, which aired on ABC's "This Week." "It's a moment that we are now really going after those tough challenges and historical problems that we fought for many years to be in the driver's seat. "

https://www.yahoo.com/gma/black-mayors-call-public-safety

Daniel J. Myers, Ph.D.

(?…What happened to all the rest of those 5,000 black race riots?…..)

Note; {When I ran across this news article during my research I was instantly stunned. Yes, the high numbers of riots shook me but that was not my main concern. The question that formulated in my mind was, ''How could thousands of race riots be 'missing' from America's history?''

I was doubly shocked that Professor Dan Myers was never told of these facts of Americans turbulent past by any teacher, professor, classmate or News Media outlet that he was exposed to for all his years of life and schooling. Add this to the fact that this is his professional line of study. But yet, he didn't know anything about these large numbers of race riots in America, until as the article says, he found out 'almost by accident'.

My first thought was the word "Conspiracy"! But this word is so over-used that I myself doubted it. After all, America is not the old USSR. America does not, could not have written out of history, thousands of race riots, just to ensure better race relations, pave the way for a black US President, (obama) and protect the legitimacy of the Civil Rights Laws, could it? Or did it?

Before we get all riled up, we must remember that Notre Dame University is a Catholic institution and thus a member of the Civil Rights Coalition. This entire group, along with all its members would have a vested interest in re-writing the most shocking and violent aspects of their movement 'out of history'. Or in other words, to 'delete' unfavorable 'facts' from the history books.

Yes, it is easy to see how these facts could have been intentionally non-taught to a younger Dan Myers during his years in the Catholic educational system. But any casual investigation will show that even the public educational system, even through college, does not mention this violent part of Americas history.

My next stop was the FBI. If there was any place in America that would have a record of all these race riots it must be at the FBI. After all is not a race riot a 'crime'? But my search of the FBIs web site brought up nothing. It is as if nothing of this nature ever happened in America.
The reason for this historical deletion is obvious, 'better race relations' in America. As most Americans would approve of this 'omission' for its practicality, is without question but…

But the bigger question still remains. Should a few People of Power control the information of the past with the intention of controlling the decisions/actions of Americas future? And is this the limit of their actions or just the tip of the iceberg? AFC

Continued Lemberg News story……………………………..
"This will give us a better picture of what was going on," he said.

Race riots were part of the volatile fabric of the mid-'60s. Anyone old enough to watch TV at the time will recall footage on the national news of stores ablaze and the bloody faces of rioters and police officers alike.

A riot that began Aug. 11, 1965, in the south central Los Angeles neighborhood of Watts resulted in 34 dead, 1,000 injured and 4,000 arrested.

Two major riots followed in 1967. A three-day free-for-all in Newark, N.J., in mid-July resulted in 26 dead, 1,100 injured and 1,600 under arrest. Two weeks later, in Detroit, a riot left a death toll of 43.

For Myers, 34, riots carry no personal interest. He was born in Xenia, Ohio, after the Watts riot and was still in diapers during the Newark and Detroit riots.

He started looking into race disturbances as an undergraduate at Ohio State University. His interest grew, and he was working on his doctorate at the University of Wisconsin when he heard murmurs of a vast collection of documents on race riots.

He made inquiries but was unable to find this legendary archive.

But after he moved to Notre Dame in 1977, he received a phone call that unraveled the mystery. The answer was to be found at Manchester College in North Manchester, Ind.

Brandeis, a Jewish-sponsored school just outside of Boston, had received gift money that allowed it to open the Lemberg Center for the Study of Violence. From 1966 to 1973, the center compiled newspaper clippings, taped interviews and paid for a Roper Poll study about race riots.

By 1973, racial violence was becoming less common, and the Lemberg Center closed.

A story in The Justice, the Brandeis student newspaper, from Sept. 18, 1973, attributed the closing to a decrease in funding and a sense that the center had completed its task.

There also was concern in the Brandeis community that information gathered at **_Lemberg_** would be used to help (white) mayors "put down riots and further oppress city (Black) populations," The Justice reported.

(Yes, it would seem the **_Lemberg_** archive was 'lost' intentionally. AFC)

In any case, the center closed and the archive suddenly had no home. "For a time, all this was stuffed under a stairwell at Brandeis," Myers said.

Eliot Wilczek, archives assistant at Brandeis, said there was no formal university archive then. He said the decision to transfer the materials on permanent loan to Manchester College, affiliated with the Church of the Brethren, was made in 1979.

Ferne Baldwin, the longtime archivist at Manchester, said the college probably seemed like the logical place for the materials.

"They came here primarily because we had the first peace studies major in America." she said. "It was quite a large collection, and it was here a long time."

But it was a little-known resource, used only by a handful of researchers." "When Notre Dame expressed an interest, we were quite willing to let them have it," Baldwin said.

One of Myers' sources told him about the Manchester collection. "When I called and asked about it, the person who answered the phone said she could see it from where she was sitting," he said.

When he rushed down to see it, he wasn't disappointed.

He's worked out an agreement involving Brandeis, Manchester and Notre Dame that leaves the archives under his care.

It's been quite a task sorting and organizing the materials.

Thousands of yellowing newspaper clippings from papers all over the country now are arranged in file cabinets in a Flanner Hall office. Each clip provides nuggets of information about an event that could be researched.

Lemberg staff members also recorded extensive interviews in 10 American cities– on reel-to-reel tapes as well as cassettes– that need to be examined.

The center also paid the Roper polling organization to interview 6,000 Americans about race relations and civil unrest.   End

"The point is that we are all capable of believing things which we know to be untrue, and then, when we are finally proved wrong, impudently twisting the facts so as to show that we were right. Intellectually, it is possible to carry on this process for an indefinite time: the only check on it is that sooner or later a false belief bumps up against solid reality, usually on a battlefield." **George Orwell**

Why the Lies? Why the Deletion out of History?

Simple, any 'law' passed under 'Duress', IE; the 'Threat of Violence' is illegal and unenforceable.

It is this point of law that made the White liberals re-write US History.

This is 'why' you have never heard any of this from your 'liberal' US History teacher.

Fun Note; The Civil Rights Law's <u>re-introduced Slavery back into American Society,</u> as it Forced White People to serve Blacks, against their will. Thus, destroying their Freedom of Choice, Freedom of Association, as well as the notion of private property. As being Forced to serve against your will, is the very definition of what 'Slavery' is all about.

THAT was the reason the Founding Fathers restricted Voting so very much. To keep the Power to make a GOD/Government OUT of the Hands of Natural-Born-Slaves!

NOTE: Affirmative Action. Diversity. Inclusion. WOKE, CRT, Set-a-Sides, Etc. would ALL be illegal IF White Men had any Civil Rights OR even the 14th Amendment, (Equal Protection of the Laws).

WHY do Blacks, (13% Pop.) Rule over America?
You must remember that Women's Rights, Gay Rights, Jewish Rights, Latino Rights, Disabled Rights, etc. etc. are all aspects of, or part of, the 5,000 black race riot Imposed, Civil Rights Laws (AKA: Black Supremacy) passed during the 1960's.

Thus, any 'attack' on the validity, or legality, of the Civil Rights Laws themselves (as with asking questions about those 5,000 race riots, 250,000 Fires used to bring America down, and pass those CR laws) would also be an Attack on 'their' Special Powers and Special Privileges.

[Remember; Any 'law' passed under 'Duress', IE; the 'Threat of Violence' is illegal and unenforceable.]

IE: Those Special Powers, Special Privileges granted by the Government, that these groups use against their enemies, (AKA: Straight, White, Male, Protestants) every day.
So, for their own benefit, the majority of White Americans <u>MUST support Black Supremacy</u> over America in order to 'protect' THEIR Special Powers and Special Privileges.
Yes, today, blacks have the vast majority of White Americans, as their 'willing' servants. Willing Slaves!
Now 'THAT' is Karma!

Or, simply put.

America's WAR against the White Man succeeded. America was defeated and re-formed under its current Marxist Government/Society.

Note. Most Americans Love living Outside the US Constitution. The Constitution was written by those 'Evil' White Men and Slave owners you know. And thus, do not represent the Will of the New and Improved non-White Man (sample shown) America.

Just remember that for 350 Years before the Civil Rights Act of 1964, Americans were Free to hire those they choose and to serve those they Choose.

They were their own Masters and did not have a federal gun to their heads, (as they do today) to force them to be just a Serf working in a government shop.

All these racist-sexist, Freedom destroying, civil rights laws, with their Special Powers and Special Privileges for Blacks and Women, Jews, Homosexuals, etc. were passed to stop blacks from burning America to the Ground, with their

5,000 race riots, 250,000 race riot fires. 1963-1973. …..
AKA: Terrorist Appeasement Laws!

Replying to @RobertGoldman
I never said that Jews didn't have some of the Best Minds in the World. I mean, to conquer, with a Black Army, an entire Nation, and have only a handful of People even knowing it ever happened was Pure Genius!

"Historians are dangerous and capable of turning everything upside down. They have to be watched."

Nikita Khrushchev
Leader of the old Soviet Union.

I would very much like to think so. AFC

"During times of universal deceit, telling the truth becomes a revolutionary act." — George Orwell

The World of the 1950's-1960's.

"Whether you like it or not, history is on our side. We will bury you!"

Nikita Khrushchev, Soviet Union Leader
(18 November 1956)

It was a time when the fate of the World was balanced on the edge of a <u>radioactive knife</u>.

It was a time when one wrong move, one wrong word, <u>could end all Humankind</u>.

It was at this 'perfect moment in history', when the enemy of the Black Race was <u>deadly vulnerable,</u> that the indomitable spirit of Malcolm X arose from the ghetto.

His passionate words of POWER, FIRE, WEALTH and FREEDOM from White Man's Rule, inspired Americas most <u>devastating Race War</u>.

This Jihad this was so powerful, so bloody, so destructive, so successful, so utterly terrifying in every way to White America, that it is <u>not spoken of</u> for fear of starting, it all over again!   AFC

A very Fun NOTE:

Hitler and MLK were SOUL Brothers!
The Civil Rights Movement against White Men and Hitler's Movement against the Jews were virtually the same thing!
……..
Hitler made WAR against the Jews in the name of Racial Equality…..
MLK made War against White Men in the name of Racial Equality…..
Both Movements involved massive Violence as the Majority (78% in America) of a Nation make WAR upon a Minority (22% Straight, White Male, Protestants).
A Minority that had toooo much $Wealth$ and Power, in the eyes of the majority.
Just change Jew to White Man and todays America instantly becomes 1930's Germany.

"I know it is the fashion to say that most of recorded history is lies anyway. I am willing to believe that history is for the most part inaccurate and biased, but what is peculiar to our own age is the abandonment of the idea that history could be truthfully written."   **George Orwell**

Truth? Who's Truth? …. ??... In a Nation where ONLY 1 in 100 even knows that Blacks committed 5,000 race riots, 250,000 fires 1963-1973, and put the US Military into Race mutiny during Vietnam and the Cold War, to 'win' those civil rights laws. IE; Terrorist laws.
How can such Massive and intentional, Government-Mandated, ignorance be overcome?
How can the Truth, ANY Truth, Prevail?

"I once said, 'We will bury you,' and I got into trouble with it. Of course we will not bury you with a shovel. Your own working class will bury you."
     Nikita Khrushchev

"America is the last stronghold of white supremacy.
The Black revolution, which is international in nature and scope, is sweeping down upon America like a raging forest fire.
It is only a matter of time before America herself will be engulfed by the Black flames, these Black firebrands."
     Malcolm X,
   Minister of Islam (The Black Muslims)
     April 17, 1961

Note 1: As this book will show, Blacks committed 5,000 race riots, 250,000 fires 1963-1973, and put the US Military into Race Mutiny during Vietnam and the Cold War, to 'win' those Civil Rights laws and with it, 'win' Black Supremacy over America.

Note;... Parts of Washington DC, were still BURNING as President Johnson, (LBJ) signed the SURENDER TERMS, (Yet another Civil Rights law) to these Black Supremacist. AKA: the "Fair Housing Act of 1968" into Law, on *April 11, 1968.*

From Congressional Record, Vol. 114, Pg. 9751, *April 11, 1968.*
As Washington DC Burned.
Hon. John R. Rarick of Louisiana.
"Mr. Speaker, the burning of our nation's capital has destroyed an estimated 600 buildings at an estimated loss of $13 million.

While the destruction was wide-spread, the "soul brothers" passed over--the burned-out area, if combined is estimated at 500 square blocks, or would form an area 20 blocks by 25 blocks.

This is Washington DC alone----a city that has not been burned by a military enemy since the British...."

It was/is a WAR, not a Movement! ….. Example; Democrats used Terrorist Attacks against America to Gain ALL those Special Powers of the Civil Rights Laws. Powers that they use against their Enemies, Straight, White, Male, Protestant, each and Every Day!

This picture shows Bobby Kennedy shaking hands with one of the Black Terrorists that had just BURNED down 500 square blocks of Washington DC, April 1968.

The Jewish Conquest of America.

In the Service of Israel and their GOD.
Jews are destroying their Centuries old Enemy, the White Man.
Thus, Conquering the Western World.

To accomplish this mighty feat, Jews gathered all those Groups in America that Hated/Envied the White Man and called it the Civil Rights Movement.
$$$$$ had less to do with it than HATRED as this Primal Human emotion, is an aspect of Humanity that is a Much More Powerful Driving Force than mere Greed!

Thus, the Civil Rights Movement was Not about giving 'Freedoms' to a 'Minority' group (14%, Blacks).
It was all about the 'Majority' <u>(78%, AKA: The Civil Rights Coalition)</u>, which was made up of Women, Blacks, Jews, Catholics, Homosexuals, etc. using 5,000 Black race riots,

250,000 Fires and putting the US Military into Race Mutiny during Vietnam, (costing America the War and the 'Waste' of 58,400 American lives,) to destroy the Freedoms and Political/Economic Powers of a minority group, <u>(22%, AKA: Straight, White, Male, Protestants).</u>

Freedoms and Political/Economic Powers that got in the Majority's way of gaining vast Wealth, Special Powers and Special Privileges for themselves.

Draconian Powers that had never before been seen on American soil.

Example: …. "Equality?"

White People Never had the government-backed 'Right'
to Force a business to Hire him.
To Force a business to Serve him.
To Force a homeowner to sell him their Home.
To Force a college to accept them!
But ALL other people and races have this Special Power.
This 5,000 black race riot imposed, "Black Supremacy"!
This "Black Aristocracy!"

Well, simply put, the Jews created, lead and as always, controlled the Civil Rights Movement.
That Blacks and their endless thousands of Terrorist acts against America are the '"" Military Wing""', of the Civil Rights Movement, is without question.

This Democratic/Jewish, Military Force took Down/conquered the US Government (5,000 black race riots, 250,000 Fires and a US Military in Race Mutiny) and re-formed Americas Society into its own (Marxist) image.

Now the Jews have control of the Full Economic and Military power of America. ALL, to serve the needs of Israel.

IE: All those endless $Billions$ in Cash, endless Billions in State-of-the-Art Weapons and of course, all those nuclear weapons, that America has given to Israel.

AND, most importantly, let's not forget all the Wars/Invasions America has done in the last few decades in the service of Israel.
Just have a look and see how many of those Wars/invasions were also the Enemies of Israel.

That the <u>US is a Vassal of Israel</u>, by every definition, is without question. AFC

US FORCES HAVE INVADED 14 ISLAMIC COUNTRIES SINCE 1980

Iran
Libya
Lebanon
Kuwait
Iraq
Somalia

Bosnia
Saudi Arabia
Afghanistan
Sudan
Kosovo
Yemen
Pakistan
Syria

JUST WHO ARE THE REAL TERRORISTS ?

[A little History here I think, as I would not want you, my reader, to think that I made all 'that' up.]

[The Jewish Conquest of America.............
Jews CREATED the Civil Rights Movement]
American Jews played a significant role in the founding and funding of some of the most important civil rights organizations, including the National Association for the Advancement of Colored People (NAACP), the Leadership Conference on Civil and Human Rights, the Southern Christian Leadership Conference (SCLC) and the Student Nonviolent Coordinating Committee (SNCC). In 1909, Henry Moscowitz joined W.E.B. DuBois and other civil rights leaders to found the NAACP. Kivie Kaplan, a vice-chairman of the Union of American Hebrew Congregations (now the Union for Reform Judaism), served as the national president of the NAACP from 1966 to 1975. Arnie Aronson worked with A. Philip Randolph and Roy Wilkins to found the Leadership Conference.

[Jews Trained their Black Army to be Loyal to THEM!]
From 1910 to 1940, more than 2,000 primary and secondary schools and twenty Black colleges (including Howard, Dillard and Fisk universities) were established in whole or in part by contributions from Jewish philanthropist Julius Rosenwald. At the height of the so-called

"Rosenwald schools," nearly forty percent of southern Blacks were educated at one of these institutions.

[Jews LEAD Blacks in their Open WAR against the 'Evil' White Man.]
During the Civil Rights Movement, Jewish activists represented a disproportionate number of whites involved in the struggle. Jews made up half of the young people who participated in the Mississippi Freedom Summer in 1964. Leaders of the Reform Movement were arrested with Rev. Dr. Martin Luther King, Jr. in St. Augustine, Florida, in 1964 after a challenge to racial segregation in public accommodations. Most famously, Rabbi Abraham Joshua Heschel marched arm-in-arm with Dr. King in his 1965 March on Selma.

https://rac.org/issues/civil-rights-voting-rights/brief-history-jews-and-civil-rights-movement-1960s

[Today's America is a Jewish-Created Nation.]
The Civil Rights Act of 1964 and the Voting Rights Act of 1965 were drafted in the conference room of Religious Action Center of Reform Judaism, under the aegis of the Leadership Conference which for decades was located in the RAC's building.

In Fact: Civil Rights and the Arthur and Sara Jo Kobacker Building

For 30 years, the Religious Action Center housed a number of key civil rights and Jewish organizations who met regularly to mobilize support for civil rights legislation. The following are a sampling of some of the key civil rights bills that were either drafted at the Center and/or for which the coalition supporting the legislation held their meetings in the Center's conference room:

- Civil Rights Act of 1964
- Voting Rights Act 1965
- Americans with Disabilities Act 1982
- Voting Rights Extension
- Japanese American Redress Act
- Civil Rights Restoration Act
- Fair Housing Act Amendments of 1988
- Civil Rights Act 1991
- https://rac.org/issues/civil-rights-voting-rights/brief-history-jews-and-civil-rights-movement-1960s

THE JEWISH ROLE
http://home.ddc.net/ygg/rj/index.htm

http://home.ddc.net/ygg/rj/rj-20.htm
ISRAEL COHEN (1912)

"We must realize that our party's most powerful weapon is racial tensions. By propounding into the consciousness of the dark races that for centuries they have been oppressed by whites, we can mold them to the program of the Communist Party. In America we will aim for subtle victory. While inflaming the Negro minority against the whites, we will endeavor to instill in the whites a guilt complex for their exploitation of the Negros. We will aid the Negroes to rise in prominence in every walk of life, in the professions and in the world of sports and entertainment. With this prestige, the Negro will be able to intermarry with the whites and begin a process which will deliver America to our cause."

Israel Cohen, A Racial Program for the Twentieth Century, 1912. Also in the Congressional Record, Vol. 103, p. 8559, June 7, 1957

The Most Important Reason for the US Government's surrender to Black Terrorism.

For those wondering what the vaulted US Military was doing as America was being Burned to the Ground by those 5,000 black race riots, 250,000 race riot fires, 1963-1973, well they had their own problems as the assassinations of White military officers by black 'servicemen' was costing America Vietnam and the 'waste' of 58,400 American lives.

How the US Government lost control of its Military and thus, Lost control of America.

Fear of Black "Street" Army
By Glen Ford, Co-publisher, The Black Commentator.

Black soldiers shut down the war (Vietnam).

The Times concedes the Black casualties were high "in the early stages of the American ground war in 1965 and 1966, when there were large numbers Blacks in front-line combat units." Here, the historical revision begins, Army and Marine

Corps commanders later took steps to reassign Black servicemen to other jobs to equalize deaths, according to Col. Harry G. Summers Jr. In "Vietnam War Almanac. "By the end of the war," said the Times, "African-Americans had suffered 12.5 percent of the total deaths in Vietnam, 1 percentage point less than their proportion in the overall population, Colonel Summers wrote."

Colonel Summers and the New York Times are talking nonsense. It is laughable to pretend that U.S. military brass acted at any time to limit Black casualty rates-What? In order to increase white death rates? Commanders "took steps to reassign Black servicemen" because African American soldiers collectively resisted Washington's plans to make them the expendable casualties of Vietnam. They effectively shut down the war from within - a history that has never been fully told. But one that is seared in the memories of those in charge of America's current and future imperial enterprises.

Despite horrendous Black casualties in the early Vietnam years, a whiter casualty list was the last thing on the Pentagon's mind. President Lyndon Johnson and Secretary of Defense Robert McNamara were most concerned about how to pull off a massive increase in U.S. troop strength without dipping too deeply into the white middle-class youth pool.

So, in 1966 a year that began with 200,000 men in Vietnam, Secretary McNamara announced Project 100,000, the most cynical race-class ploy ever lumped under the umbrella of LBJ's War on Poverty. As Defense Department manpower official Dr. Wayne S. Sellman explained to congressional committee in February 1990.

"The manpower goal of Project 100,000 was to accept 40,000 men under relaxed standards during the 1st year and 100,000 per year thereafter. Approximately 91 percent of these "New Standards Men," as they were called, came in under lowered aptitude/education standards, and 9 percent

entered under lowered physical standards."

With a straight face, Secretary McNamara declared that Project 100,000 was intended for the benefit of the 'poor of American (who) have not had the opportunity to earn their fair share of this Nation's abundance but they can be given any opportunity to serve in their Country's defense" Military testing standards were lowered, high school dropouts became eligible for service, and draft boards and recruiters were encouraged to overlook criminal justice offenses.

By 1971, when the U.S. ground war in Vietnam was sputtering to an end, "354,000 L/A men had entered the Services under the program," Dr. Sellman testified. "Of these, 54 percent were volunteers and 46 percent were draftees. The men who entered under Project 100,000 were on average 20 years of age, about half came from the South, and a substantial proportion , about 41 percent, were minorities."

This was the infusion that allowed the Pentagon to boost Vietnam troop strength to 540,000 in peak year of 1969, while accommodating massive draft deferments among the comfortable white classes. Young Black draftees and volunteers flocked to elite outfits, comprising near or absolute majorities in "line" units of the 101st and 82nd Airborne Divisions and the 173rd Airborne brigade.

There was one problem with this Black "street" army. As a Black lieutenant put it in "Bloods," Wallace Terry's seminal oral history of African Americans in Vietnam, "They are the ones who ain't going to take no shit."

The "commanders" that war historian Col. Summers credits with compassionately reassigning Blacks out of harms way in fact went to extreme lengths to break the spirits of Black soldiers and destroy any expressions of Black solidarity. Ultimately, the military established a mostly Black penal colony in Vietnam to enforce the terms of its internal race war.

An online History of the Military Police cites 1969 as the "year the US military prisoner population peaks when 10,450 military prisoners are confined in Vietnam, most at the United States, Army Installation Stockade at Long Binh, known as the Long Binh Jail (LBJ)."

In August 1968, Black inmates burned Long Minh Jail to the ground, Jimi Childress was 19 years old, locked up for going AWOL from his unit. He told his story to Cecil Barr Currey, author of "Long Binh Jail: An Oral History of Vietnam's Notorious

U.S. Military Prison. (1999).

"I can recall at one time they had eight of us in one (6' x 9' x 6' metal) conex box, A slit in the front and a slit in the back- and that was your air. And if you wanted to urinate, you had to go to the back to do it because they kept a chain on the front with a lock on it. This was in heat of more than 115 degrees. You could see them treating prisoners that way, but not their own soldiers......

"All these guys that was in these conex boxes were Black. You See? White guys in the stockade had fringe benefits. We had none. It was just a hateful place. Hispanics stuck with Blacks, just for safety reason, but there was so few you hardly notice. It was a Black prison. I will never forget how many Blacks were incarcerated in that stockade."

In 1968, combined Vietnam AWOLs and desertions reached over 150 per thousand soldiers. About 100 Black deserters established "Soul Alley" in a Saigon neighborhood near Ton San Nhut Airport. Fully armed Black and white troops faced off at China Beach, Danang.

The online military police site sketches the rough outlines of repression and resistance in Vietnam. Some entrees from 1971:

. September 1971 - Military police conduct a siege at Cam Ranh Bay against 14 soldiers of the 35th Engineer Group who refuse to come out of their bunkers.

. October 9, 1971 - First Cavalry troopers again commit a "combat refusal" when asked to form a patrol. (This was an integrated affair, as were many, but not most, fraggings.)

. October 1971 - Military police are flown into a military

base near DaLat, after two fragging attempts had been made on the commanding officer's life. Discipline is restored after the MP's have been on scene for a week.

By the end of the year there were 333 incidents of fragging reported in Vietnam.

The MP's give credence to a "fragging" study by historian Terry Anderson of Texas A & M University." "The US Army itself does not know exactly how many ...(White) officers were murdered. But they know at least 600 were murdered, and then they have another 1400 that died mysteriously, consequently by early 1970, the army (was) at war not with the enemy but with itself. The internal "war" was overwhelming racial in character."

(We will never know exactly how of those names on "the Wall" were put there because of the Jihad (race war) of Malcolm X, but it will be many thousands.)

Racism gets a beat down;
"We had only one mission in Washington: to prevent the white troops from doing harm to Black civilians."

But there they were, the assembled men of GAWD, three days after King's murder, inventing, right there on the spot, the myth of the Black church as Dr. King's stalwart soldiers in the army of social change in the South – when the truth was, for the most part, diametrically the opposite.

Monday morning, I was back at Fort Bragg. The fires had been raging all weekend in a hundred cities – although not Columbus, Georgia. I and other stragglers caught up with our unit in Washington, DC, where the officers already knew the street layout from their map studies out in the field just days before. The brothers of the 82nd Airborne Division considered that we had only one mission in Washington: to prevent the white troops from doing harm to Black civilians. There would be no repeat of the white New Jersey National Guard's lynch mob behavior in occupying Newark , New Jersey, a year earlier.

We were at war stateside, as well, I was among the 6,000 soldiers of the 82nd Airborne Division that occupied Washington, DC in the aftermath of Dr. Martin Luther King's assassination, April 1968. Black troops made up about half of the division's line units. We were aware that the near-lily white New Jersey National Guard had gone on killing rampage on the streets of Newark the previous year, and we made it unmistakably clear to white soldiers that no harm was to come to the DC (Black) population. Nobody got hurt.

At "home" in Fort Bragg, North Carolina, we bloodied the Division's overwhelmingly white and southern MP's at every nocturnal opportunity. While the Ku Klux Klan and other racist groups ran amuck at nearby Camp Lejeune Marine Base, racists at Fort Bragg sulked in silence. Criminal investigation Detachment personnel enter Black-dominated barracks in force, if at all.

In the fall of 1966, Commanding General John Deane,

weary of racial strife, called the entire division to a parade field. "I give up," he said, bluntly, then pledge to address a long list of Black grievances. He kept most of those promises. The Black soldiers of the 82nd had the "critical mass" to kick ass, if provoked. End.   Glen Ford.

https://Blackcommentator.com/ebooks_menu.php

Note: [Since the end of the draft in 1973 the U.S. military has succeeded in whitening the combat arms by excluding low test scorers, high school dropouts, and people with criminal records--a huge chunk of African American youth. (Twelve percent of Black males in their 20s and early 30s are in jail or prison on any given day.)] Glen Ford.

OCTOBER 30, 2008
Turning the Tide of Ethnic Cleansing in America's Cities

BY GLEN FORD at Glen.Ford@BlackAgendaReport.com

You may ask, "Why didn't the US Constitution, stop America from becoming a Marxist Aristocracy?" Simple, the US Constitution was just Ignored.

America Loves to live outside the US Constitution....
Example;
""Nearly 70% of Americans believe Roe v. Wade shouldn't be overturned."''"....... And it is "THIS'", (70%) that caused an obviously illegal 'Law' or 'Right", to exist all these years. Just like those illegal Civil Rights Laws.
Yes, the Civil Rights Laws are illegal, just like R vs W, is illegal.......
Note; Any 'law' passed under 'Duress', IE; the 'Threat of Violence' is illegal and unenforceable.....
And Blacks committed 5,000 race riots, 250,000 fires 1963-1973, and put the US Military into Race mutiny during Vietnam and the Cold War, to 'win' those civil rights laws. IE; Terrorist laws.
Thus, all these Civil Rights Laws are illegal.
But today, with 78% of Americans directly or indirectly $benefiting$ from the 'Heart and Soul' of the Democratic Party, the Special POWERS and Special Privileges of those Civil Rights Laws.
Laws that they use against their Enemies, straight, White, Male, Protestants, each and every day.
It is VERY easy for Americans to 'overlook, forget, ignore, lie, delete, distort, re-write, Etc.', the Historical FACT, that every last Civil Rights Law, is based on Capitulation to Terrorism and Mad efforts at Terrorist appeasement.

But back to R vs W, This Law/Right was MADE, Created by the USSC as it is not based upon any pre-existing Law nor any aspect of the US Constitution.... NOTE: The USSC has NO Constitutional Power to Create Law.
These are just 2 examples of how America's Majority Ignores the US Constitution whenever it suits them.

THAT was the reason the Founding Fathers restricted Voting so very much. To keep the Power to make a GOD/Government OUT of the Hands of Natural-Born-Slaves!

Note; Any 'Democracy' that Destroys Freedom and Creates an Aristocracy, NEEDS to be destroyed!
White People Never had the government-backed 'Right'
To Force a business to Hire him.
To Force a business to Serve him.
To Force a homeowner to sell him their Home.
To Force a College to accept them!
But ALL other people and races have this Special Power.
This 5,000 black race riot imposed, "Black Supremacy!"'
This 5,000 black race riot imposed, "Black Aristocracy!"

Excerpt from book, "Ebony OZ: How the Jihad of Malcolm X, WON Black Homelands in America".

YES, the "Masters of the World" were KICKED OUT of the 'JEWELS' of America by the fury and fire and the FEAR of the BLACK RACE!"

Before 1967 no major American city ever had a Black mayor, ever! But in 1967 Carl Stokes became the first Black mayor of Cleveland Ohio and Richard Hatcher won Gary Indiana's mayoral election. By 1973 there were 48 Black mayors in 48, newly made, Black homelands, (not that the white devils would ever admit losing them in the first place, ever!), by 1990 it was 316 to over 400 by 1998 AND AT LAST COUNT OVER 640 Black Homelands all across America!

From 0 to over 640 American cities now Black homelands in UNDER 40 years! The very real results, of the very real, GREAT JIHAD, of the very real and very GREAT, Malcolm X!
His greatest dream come true, the Black race in America, under Black rule! Real BLACK POWER in all its GLORY!

Fun Note: Forced Public School integration was, and still is, a great 'tool' that Blacks used to Ethnically Cleanse Americas cities of their White Populations.

''I once said, 'We will bury you,' and I got into trouble with it. Of course we will not bury you with a shovel. Your own working class will bury you.''
    Nikita Khrushchev

"America is the last stronghold of white supremacy.
The Black revolution, which is international in nature and scope, is sweeping down upon America like a raging forest fire.
It is only a matter of time before America herself will be engulfed by the Black flames, these Black fire brands.
Malcolm X,
  Minister of Islam (The Black Muslims)
    April 17, 1961

Note; **United States Supreme Court Justices were in Hiding in their Bunkers as Democrats/Blacks/Terrorists rioted, Looted and BURNED 500 square blocks of Washington DC along with 125 other Cities.. April 1968,**

ALL to Force passage of the Fair Housing Act, that Forced the Government to FORCE White People to allow Blacks, to live in their Neighborhoods.
And this Obvious Terrorist imposed Law, is STILL Law over America today!
Why?... FEAR!   As any mention of revoking the civil rights laws, because they are Terrorist imposed, would cause massive Chaos and uncountable death and destruction of America.

"Poverty frees them from ordinary standards of behavior, just as money frees people from work."
— George Orwell

Reminder because it is Very Important;

Yes, 5,000 black race riots and 250,000 Fires were used to Create and pass those Civil Rights Laws………
But today, with 78% of Americans directly or indirectly $benefiting$ from the 'Heart and Soul' of the Democratic Party, the Civil Rights Laws. It is <u>VERY</u> easy for Americans to 'overlook, forget, ignore, lie, delete, distort, re-write, Etc.', the Historical FACT, that every last Civil Rights Law, is based on Capitulation to Terrorism and Mad efforts at Race Riot appeasement.
 (Just like today with Black Lives Matter).
Also, note that every Civil Rights Law is based on the destruction of Freedom in America.

A reminder;
Even though all these thousands of black race riots and hundreds of thousands of race riot Fires have been Deleted out of Americas history, so as to 'Protect' the legitimacy of those Wildly Popular, but Race Riot Imposed, Civil Rights Laws.

As any 'law' passed under 'Duress', IE; the 'Threat of Violence' is illegal and unenforceable.

It is this point of law that made the White liberals, re-write US History. This is 'why' you have never heard any of this from your 'liberal' US History teacher.

Fun Note; The Civil Rights Law's' <u>re-introduced Slavery back into American Society,</u> as it Forced White People to serve Blacks, against their wills. Thus, destroying their Freedom of Choice, Freedom of Association, as well as the notion of private property. As being Forced to serve against your will, is the very definition of what 'Slavery' is all about.

"The choice for mankind lies between freedom and happiness and for the great bulk of mankind, happiness is better." — George Orwell

Fun Note; **When those "liberals" used those 5,000 black race riots, 250,000 Fires, and put the US Military into Race Mutiny, during Vietnam and the Cold War, 1963-1973, to bring the US Government to its knees and install a 'New Society', in their own image, just as Hitler did in Europe, they became fascist and so did the government, as it needed fascist powers to enforce those Freedom destroying, civil rights laws.**

Very Fun Note;

**John Wilkes Booth Really made the USA PAY for its conquest of the Confederacy, didn't he? As killing Lincoln Stopped Lincoln's Plans for Moving all the freed Blacks to Central America. Thus, all those 5,000 Black race riots, those (250,000) BLACK FIRES from Americas BURNING Cities. All those destroyed Freedoms. GOD/Government, controlling our every move, in the name of "Equality".
30 MILLION White people were forced to flee America's BURNING cities.**

Freedoms lost, that Americas had once fought and died to protect for 250 years, All destroyed by those very same Black slave descendants, that could have been living happily in Belize, IF it were not for actions of one, (1) man.

Yes, I feel that IF Lincoln could have seen the way blacks were Rioting, Looting and BURNING 500 square blocks of Washington DC along with 125 other American cities, April 1968, he never would have fought the CSA to end black slavery at the cost of 620,000 White men's lives.

Definition of Terrorism
: the use of violent acts to frighten the people in an area as a way of trying to achieve a political goal.

From the Congressional Record, Vol. 114, Pg. 9534, April 10, 1968. As Washington DC Burned.
Congressman Tuck of Virginia.

"The horrendous situation which now exists is accentuated by what appears to be a complete and abject surrender of the executive and legislative departments of our government to these ruthless racists, looters, thieves and incendiarists whose real object is to pillage and plunder and also destroy the Government of the United States."

Father Harold's "Key Words".

"It's a beautiful thing, the destruction of words."— **George Orwell**

"But if thought corrupts language, language can also corrupt thought." **George Orwell**

First of all, I will do as my old College Logic Professor, Father Harold, always taught us about logical Debates and writings, "Establish mutually agreed upon definitions of your 'Key' Words." This is very important as you will see as the very definitions of many Very Important 'Words' have been changed 180 degrees to mean exactly the opposite of what they did all those years ago.

"The Revolution will be complete when the language is perfect." — George Orwell

FREEDOM

Even the word <u>Freedom</u> has been changed from meaning being your own 'Master' and in control of your life and Property, to mean something evil and 'Dirty', called, 'Discrimination'.

For 350 Years before the Civil Rights Act of 1964, Americans were Free to hire those they choose and to serve those they Choose.

They were their own Masters and did not have a federal gun to their heads, (as they do today) to force them to be just a Serf working in a government shop.

All these racist-sexist, Freedom destroying, civil rights laws, with their Special Powers and Special Privileges for Blacks and Women, Jews, Homosexuals, etc. were passed to stop blacks from burning America to the Ground, with their 5,000 race riots, 250,000 race riot fires. 1963-1973. …..
AKA: Terrorist Appeasement Laws!

SLAVERY

'Slavery' has been Normal on Earth for the last 100,000 years. Slavery of every race and ethnic group was on every continent and It was Not Invented by White men. Black slaves were already slaves to their Black Masters in Africa. They were mostly POWs from the endless tribal wars, think Rwanda 1990s, here and would have been killed, as a danger to the tribe, without the 'Outlet' of 'slavery' to the Americas and other parts of the World.
Slavery saved the life of every black that made it to Americas shores and ALL their descendants, including the previous first lady.
ALL to the Woe of America.

Fun Note: Those 5,000 Black race riots, 250,000 Fires (1963-1973), imposed by means of Terrorist actions against America, 'the Civil Rights Laws'
re-introduced Slavery back into American Society, as it Forced White People to serve Blacks, against their wills. Thus destroying their Freedom of Choice, Freedom of Association, as being Forced to serve against your will is the very definition of what 'Slavery' is all about.

RIGHTS

The Very Meaning of "Rights" has been Changed 180 Degrees!
"RIGHTS" 200 years ago meant a Restricted Government and FREEDOMS for the People!
"RIGHTS" today means the Special Powers and Special Privileges the Government gives to selected groups of Americans to be used against their Enemies. AKA: Straight, White, Male, Protestants.
'Rights' today means Government Tyranny and Oppression of the People and the Restriction/Destruction of Peoples Freedoms.

There is no swifter route to the corruption of thought than through the corruption of language.
George Orwell

"War is peace. Freedom is slavery. Ignorance is strength." ~ George Orwell

Hitler and MLK were SOUL Brothers!

The Civil Rights Movement was/is reminiscent of Germany of the 1930's, when the majority of Germans felt that a 'Minority' (Jews) had too much Wealth and Power (also called Jealousy) and so the Majority banded together under Hitler, so as to Equalize this 'unfair', 'unequal', situation. …..That this quest for Equality and Racial Justice used massive amounts of Violence and ended with the Holocaust is a matter of history.

It was/is much the same with the Civil Rights Movement/Coalition, that represented 78% of Americas Population (Women, Jews, Blacks, Catholics, Homosexuals, etc.) and banded together under MLK and used 5,000 race riots, 250,000 Fires and put the US Military into race Mutiny during Vietnam, to Force the Government to grant Special Powers and Special Privileges to the members of the Civil Rights Coalition, to be used against their Mortal Enemies,…. AKA: Straight, White, Male, Protestants. …. A 22% Minority Group, that has no Civil Rights Protections.

In fact, just change Jew to White Man and America instantly become a 1930s Germany!

SEGREGATION

"To integrate with evil is to be destroyed with evil. What we want indeed, justice for us is to be set apart. We want, and must insist upon an area in this land that we can call our own, somewhere (where) we can hold our heads (up) with pride and dignity, without the continued harassments and indignities of our oppressors."
"The size of the territory can be judged according to our own population. If our people number one-seventh of Americas total population, then give us one-seventh of this land!"
"We must win our freedom from these blue-eyed devils by any means necessary!"   Malcolm X…Minister of the Nation of Islam

Jim Crow (AKA; Racial Segregation)

"To see what is in front of one's nose needs a constant struggle."   George Orwell

Jim Crow Laws, were White People Not wanting their cities to be Third World, un-flushed Toilets, like Detroit,

Washington DC, Chicago, Minneapolis, Birmingham, etc. etc.

Jim Crow Laws were White people Not wanting their Children to be put into Third World, Inner-city schools, filled with Gangs, Drugs, Shootings, Rapes in the bathrooms, and Violence, everywhere, in the name of 'Equality'.

As "Equally" BAD, seems to have been Liberals deliberate goals.
???.. WHY did America WANT ALL of Americas schools to be Inner-city ghetto Schools?
Just to Train Black children in how to 'Act White?'
Just to show White Children that Blacks are 'just-like-them?'

I Homeschooled My 2 Girls as "YOU PEOPLE" destroyed the Public School system, with your _Social Engineering, Madness,_ as '"Equally BAD" was/is your moto.

The picture is of Washington DC. Segregation of America's cities is Greater today than it was in 1950.
WHY?... Blacks are using Ethnic Cleansing, (Crime/Rioting/Terrorism) to take control of the Cities and ALL the JOBS, City CONTRACTS, POWER, and MONEY those cities contain!
Green is Blacks, (right side)... Blue is Whites, (Left side).

Washington DC
(Ethnic Cleansing timeline)

Ethnic Makeup of the District of Columbia[8][70]

Year	White (includes White Hispanics)	Non-Hispanic White	Black	Asian	Native Americans	Other	Hispanic or Latino (any race)
1800	69.6%	-	30.4%	-	-	-	-
1810	66.9%	-	33.1%	-	-	-	-
1950	64.6%	-	35.0%	0.4%	-	-	-
1960	45.2%	-	53.9%	0.6%	0.1%	0.2%	-
1970	27.7%	26.5%	71.1%	0.7%	0.1%	0.4%	2.1%
1980	26.9%	25.7%	70.3%	1.0%	0.2%	1.6%	2.8%

Race Riots and Ethnic Cleansing. DC

DC, from 65% White to 27%.

DC, from 35% black to 71% black.

DETROIT

{"What it showed, actually, is that revolution is possible in the United States.} The 1967 Detroit Rebellion
Revolutionary Worker #915, July 13, 1997

"Detroit's Black population today stands at about 78 percent, the highest proportion of any city in the United States. In contrast, the metro area, including Detroit, is only 23 percent Black, and 68 percent white, making Detroit the most segregated city in the United States"
"1960, Detroit's population was 29% African American, by 1970 that number was 45%, and in 2010, Detroit's population was 82.7% African American.

By 1980, not only did black people make up over 60% of the population, but the population of Detroit as a whole had decreased by 35% since its height in 1950.

When did Detroit become a majority Black city, you might ask?

1980

"Negro snipers turned 140 square blocks north of West Grand Blvd. into a bloody battlefield for three hours last night, temporarily routing police and national guardsmen.... Tanks thundered through the streets and heavy machine guns clattered....

The scene was incredible. It was as though the Viet Cong had infiltrated the riot-Blackened streets."

Excerpted from *The 1967 Detroit Rebellion Revolutionary Worker #915, July 13, 1997*

In the two years following the uprisings, it is estimated that nearly 150,000 white Detroiters fled for the suburbs. Between 1970 and 1980, Detroit flipped from a majority white city to a majority Black city." City Snapshot: Detroit | Othering & Belonging Institute

https://belonging.berkeley.edu › city-snapshot-detroit

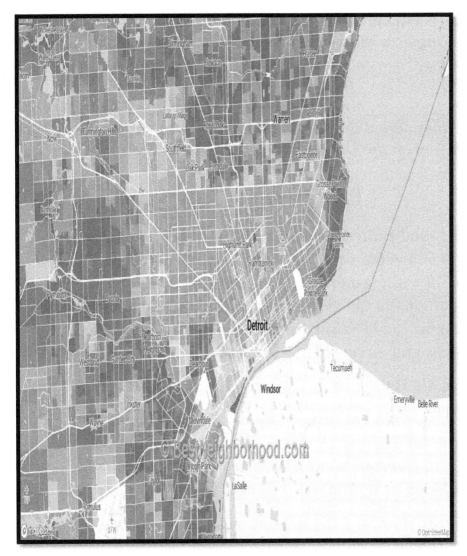

Detroit Ethnic Cleansing.

Segregation of Americas cities it Greater today than it was in 1950.
WHY?... Blacks are using Ethnic Cleansing, (Crime/Rioting/Terrorism) to take control of the Cities and ALL their POWER and MONEY!..... Green is Blacks, (center)... Blue is Whites, (outside center).

From Wikipedia, the free encyclopedia

The King assassination riots, also known as the Holy Week Uprising,[1] was a wave of civil disturbance which swept the United States following the assassination of Martin Luther King Jr. on April 4, 1968, which triggered unrest in 125 cities across the United States. It was the greatest wave of social unrest the United States had experienced since the Civil War.[2]

Baltimore

In the 1960 United States Census, Baltimore was home to 610,608 white residents, 65% of Baltimore's population. By 1970 white Americans were 53% of Baltimore's population, on the verge of becoming the minority for the first time due to White flight [Ethnic Cleansing] to the suburbs and an increasing African-American population.

When did Baltimore become mostly black?

Majority white for most of its history, Baltimore transitioned to having a black majority in the 1970s. As of the 2010 Census, African Americans are the majority population of Baltimore at 63% of the population.

From; History of African Americans in Baltimore - Wikipedia

https://en.wikipedia.org › wiki ›

Here is a snapshot of Baltimore's Ethnic Cleansing.

From;... POLITICS

The Deep, Troubling Roots of Baltimore's Decline

If we want to save Charm City, we must begin by reversing 100 years of segregation.

"Since the civil rights movement, but especially since the 1968 riots—sparked by Martin Luther King's assassination after 15 years of nonviolent protest—Baltimore has been a largely black city. This is mostly a function of population decline, stemming from the riots. From 1970 to 2000, the city's population fell by nearly one-third, from 906,000 to 651,000. At the same time, the number of black residents rose. In 1950, just 24 percent of Baltimoreans were black. By 1980, it was 54 percent, and by 2000, it was 65 percent.

Now, Baltimore is a city of 620,000, and the large majority—63.7 percent—are black"

BY JAMELLE BOUIE
APRIL 29, 2015

"Since the civil rights movement, but especially since the 1968 riots—sparked by Martin Luther King's assassination after 15 years of nonviolent protest—Baltimore has been a largely black city. This is mostly a function of population decline, stemming from the riots, [Ethnic Cleansing]. From 1970 to 2000, the city's population fell by nearly one-third, from 906,000 to 651,000. At the same time, the number of black residents rose. In 1950, just 24 percent of Baltimoreans were black. By 1980, it was 54 percent, and by 2000, it was 65 percent.

Now, Baltimore is a city of 620,000, and the large majority—63.7 percent—are black"

The Ethnic Cleansing (Segregation) of Baltimore. Blue is Whites, (outer). Green is Blacks, (Inner).

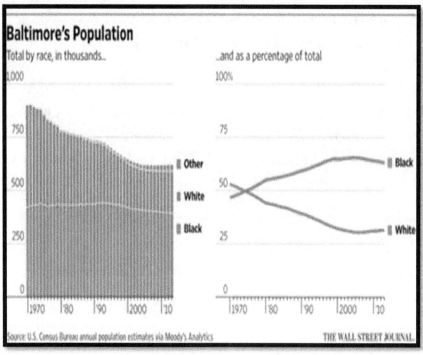

Chicago

While African Americans made up less than two percent of the city's population in 1910, by 1960 the city was nearly 25 percent black.

Looking back into historical data also shows some interesting trends – non-Hispanic whites made up 59% of the residents of Chicago in 1970, falling to just 31.7% in 2010 – which indicates that many of the people leaving the city over the past few decades for the suburbs have been from among its relatively more affluent white population.

History of African Americans in Chicago - Wikipedia

https://en.wikipedia.org › wiki ›

The largest Chicago racial/ethnic groups are White (33.1%) followed by Black (28.8%) and Hispanic (28.7%).

Here is a small sample/story of the Cancer of Chicago as Whites are Ethnically Cleansed from the city and Black Supremacy/Hispanic Supremacy, takes over the city.

[It seemed that just as soon as Black people made the neighborhood their own, its fortunes turned. Houses started falling into disrepair, thanks to disinvestment. Stores closed up shop.]

ENGLEWOOD, CHICAGO — By the time Eugene Sawyer became Chicago's mayor in 1987 following the sudden death of the first African American to hold the office, Black residents were already leaving.

For decades, long before Sawyer's ascension, the Englewood neighborhood had been a center of Black life in Chicago, boasting one of the city's busiest commercial districts and a growing middle class. And it was a true power base, a center of political gravity: Sawyer launched his political career near here, in the 6th Ward of Chicago's City Council.

But there were signs of change, even then. It seemed that just as soon as Black people made the neighborhood their own, its fortunes turned. Houses started falling into disrepair, thanks to disinvestment. Stores closed up shop — including the massive Sears store that <u>left the neighborhood</u> in 1976.

Now that trickle is a flood. Englewood, one of Chicago's 77 community areas, boasted nearly 100,000 people in 1960 but is now home to about 22,000. Like a tide going out, it has left relics of decades of decline: more abandoned buildings, shuttered schools and boarded-up storefronts. Its remaining residents face a seemingly intractable level of street violence.

Security cameras on the wall of the local Planned Parenthood, where a mural of Englewood has been painted.

On a recent November afternoon, Roderick Sawyer, who narrowly won his father's old City Council seat in 2011, walked past block after block of vacant lots, pointing out the empty homes and apartment buildings whose gutted frames were overgrown by weeds, exposing themselves to Chicago's notorious weather.

When he toured the neighborhood after his election, Sawyer said, "I'm not going to lie, I cried a little bit. I had tears in my eyes, because I saw there was nothing being paid attention in a lot of areas of Englewood."

Englewood's descent from a boomtown to a ghost town is a story with many causes, from government neglect to the loss of manufacturing jobs. But it's also a story about what happens to a neighborhood when people decide to give up and leave — and how that reshapes the city around it. [End]

https://www.politico.com/news/magazine/2021/12/07/chicago-black-population-decline-523563

Lightfoot's Chicago: Over 3,200 People Shot January Through November 2022

"**"We have started to change Chicago around for the better," Lightfoot said during a recent debate. "I want to finish the job that we have started.""**

https://www.breitbart.com/politics/2022/12/04/lightfoots-chicago-over-3200-people-shot-january-through-november-2022/

NATIONAL
Illinois' richest man ditches Chicago for Miami, says employees don't feel safe
by: John Clark
Posted: Jun 23, 2022 / 05:54 PM CDT

https://www.mystateline.com/news/national/illinois-richest-man-ditches-chicago-for-miami-says-employees-dont-feel-safe/

Says a verylot about Ethnic Cleansing in Chicago. 3,200 people shot and Businesses fleeing the city. White Businesses fleeing the city.

ABC News….. (As Crime-Rioting-Terrorism are used to Ethnically Cleanse Americas cities!)
Black mayors call public safety, homelessness biggest issues for New York, LA and Houston

MEGHAN MISTRY
Sun, January 22, 2023 at 7:08 AM PST

For the first time in history, Black mayors are leading America's four largest cities.

ABC News' Chief Washington Correspondent Jonathan Karl recently sat down with three of them -- New York City Mayor Eric Adams, Los Angeles Mayor Karen Bass and Houston Mayor Sylvester Turner -- in Washington, D.C., on the sidelines of the annual gathering of the countries' mayors.

"It's a moment for us," Adams told Karl in the interview, which aired on ABC's "This Week." "It's a moment that we are now really going after those tough challenges and historical problems that we fought for many years to be in the driver's seat."

Turner, who was first elected in 2016 and is currently serving a second term, said that while their mayoralities signal that "progress is being made," he hopes that enough Black mayors are elected "to the point where it doesn't stand out."

https://www.yahoo.com/gma/black-mayors-call-public-safety

NOTE: WHY is 80% of Americas major cities under Black Supremist Domination?.... Becoming BLACK HOODS!…..Ethnic Cleansing... is WHY!...

"The question became at what point in a city's development did enough white citizens move out to create the possibility that a Black could win?" Said Tobe Johnson, chairman of political science at Morehouse College in

Atlanta, "The phenomenon was ridiculed at the time. They (Blacks) were laughed at for taking over hopeless cities."

You will find Tobe Johnson's quote, verbatim in a Detroit News story Feb. 14, 2000 Called "Black voters give rise to leaders", by Cameron McWhirter.

Blacks committed 5,000 race riots, 250,000 fires 1963-1973, and put the US Military into Race mutiny during Vietnam and the Cold War, to 'win' those civil rights laws. IE; Terrorist laws.

THIS caused 30 MILLION White people to FLEE the Burning Cities.

This was the largest, most successful Ethnic Cleansing operation in the history of the World, as few even know it ever happened.

THIS is WHY Blacks lead Americas Major cities!

Ethnic Cleansing

Ethnic cleansing

From Wikipedia, the free encyclopedia

Ethnic cleansing is the systematic forced removal of ethnic, racial, and religious groups from a given area, with the intent of making a region ethnically homogeneous. (such as Detroit, DC, etc.)
Along with direct removal, such as extermination, deportation or population transfer, it also includes indirect methods aimed at forced migration by coercing the victim group to flee and preventing its return, such as murder, rape, and property destruction.[2][3][4]

It constitutes a <u>crime against humanity</u> and may also fall under the <u>Genocide Convention</u>, even as ethnic cleansing has no legal definition under <u>international criminal law</u>.[2][5][6]

"To integrate with evil is to be destroyed with evil. What we want indeed, justice for us is to be set apart. We want, and must insist upon an area in this land that we can call our own, somewhere (where) we can hold our heads (up) with pride and dignity, without the continued harassments and indignities of our oppressors."

"The size of the territory can be judged according to our own population. If our people number one-seventh of Americas total population, then give us one-seventh of this land!"

"We must win our freedom from these blue-eyed devils by any means necessary!   Malcolm X

"Actually, Americas most dangerous and threatening black man is the one who has been kept sealed up by the Northerner in the black ghettoes.
                            Malcolm X

Just Remember that Blacks youth commit MURDER at a Rate that is 70 Times Higher than White People......
"Racism?"..... Get REAL!
BUT Murder/Violent Crime are a Cultural IE; Trained event.
Blacks don't commit Murder at a rate that is 70 Times higher than the rate for White people, just because of the color of their skin. Just like a Tiger and its Stripes, it has to be Trained to Kill.
Just as <u>*Black Children are Trained to Kill*</u> to be Good Soldiers in the decades long Ethnic Cleansing of Americas cities.
And NOT trained to be Good Husbands and Attentive Fathers, by the way.

From The <u>Wall Street Journal</u>, on the JAMA report:
Since 1990, rates of gun-related homicide have been highest among <u>black men aged 20 to 24, the analysis said, with 142 fatalities per 100,000 people</u> in this group in 2021—a 74% increase since 2014.
Homicide rates are as much as 23 times higher among black men and as much as nearly four times higher among Hispanic men than among white men, the analysis said.
<u>http://click.heritage.org/ODI0LU1IVC0zMDQAAAGIpaZwua 9VloUDZ7UlT9ksS1mjtz6hYYyhwrVU0ynKrnFVYNIo9yR6cy k0bgnOcpKHYdnaXko=</u>

Black youth MURDER at 70Xs the rate of White Men! From The Wall Street Journal, on the JAMA report: *Since 1990, rates of gun-related homicide have been highest among black men aged 20 to 24, the analysis said, with 142 fatalities per 100,000 people in this group in 2021*

142 Blacks, age 20-24 Murder rate, @ up here. ←--

∧

130

120

Now you know HOW and WHY Blacks WON their Race WAR against the 'evil' White Man.

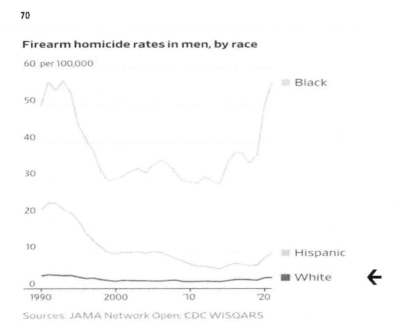

WHY are America's major cities under Black Supremacist Domination?....

Becoming BLACK HOODS!

The Democratic Party is the Party of Black People, as

Blacks are the Military Wing of the Democratic party. Why is this?...

Remember; Blacks committed 5,000 race riots, 250,000 fires 1963-1973, and put the US Military into Race mutiny during Vietnam and the Cold War, to 'win' those civil rights laws. IE; Terrorist laws.

But today, with 78% of Americans directly or indirectly $benefiting$ from the 'Heart and Soul' of the Democratic Party, the Civil Rights Laws.

Laws/Special Powers and Special Privileges they use against their Mortal ENEMIES, Straight, White, Male, Protestants, every day.

It is VERY easy for Americans to 'overlook, forget, ignore, lie, delete, distort, re-write, Etc.', the Historical FACT, that every last Civil Rights Law, is based on Capitulation to Terrorism and Mad efforts at Terrorist appeasement.

(Just like today with Black Lives Matter).

Excerpt from the book, ''Ebony OZ: How the Jihad of Malcolm X, WON Black Homelands in America''.

''YES, the "Masters of the World" were KICKED OUT of the 'JEWELS' of America by the fury and fire and the FEAR of the BLACK RACE!''

Before 1967 no major American city ever had a Black mayor, ever! But in 1967 Carl Stokes became the first Black mayor of Cleveland Ohio and Richard Hatcher won Gary Indiana's mayoral election. By 1973 there were 48 Black mayors in 48, newly made, Black homelands, (not that the white devils would ever admit losing them in the first place, ever!), by 1990 it was 316 to over 400 by 1998 AND AT LAST COUNT OVER 640 Black Homelands all across America!

From 0 to over 640 American cities now Black homelands in UNDER 40 years! The very real results, of the very real, GREAT JIHAD, of the very real and very GREAT, Malcolm X!

His greatest dream come true, the Black race in America, under Black rule! Real BLACK POWER in all its GLORY! Fun Note: Forced Public School integration was, and still is, a great 'tool' that Blacks used to Ethnically Cleanse America's cities of their White Populations.''

Ethnic Cleansing is called White Replacement today, as it is nation-wide and endlessly $Costly$.

October 09, 2023

Biden Says, AGAIN, That U.S. Will Soon Be a "Minority White" Country

By Selwyn Duke

"An unrelenting stream of immigration, nonstop, nonstop … will make white people an absolute minority in the U.S.," said then-Vice President Joe Biden in 2015. Biden has now echoed this, too, stating in a recent interview that ours will soon be "a minority-white-European country" but that, nonetheless, whites should be treated with "respect."

"We're going to be — very shortly — a minority-white European country," Biden told ProPublica in an interview published last Sunday. "And sometimes my [Democrat] colleagues don't speak enough to make it clear that that is not going to change how we operate."

Does this mean the Left will continue pushing "white privilege" theory; the "white supremacy" narrative; affirmative action and quotas disadvantaging white men; and "equity," a euphemism for government-sanctioned, politically correct discrimination? Biden didn't specify.

He did, however, emphasize that the new white minority should be treated with "respect" (video below), which may be a tacit admission that his party currently treats them with anything but.

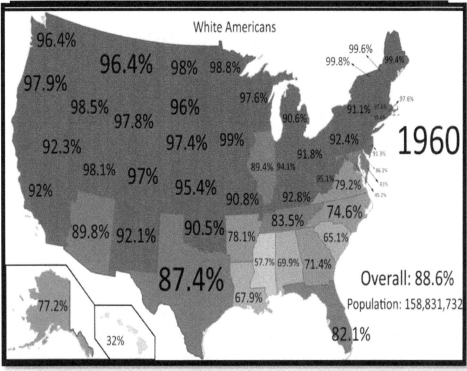
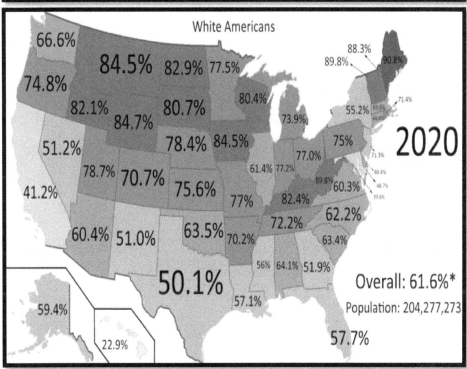

Bloomberg
Adams Begs State to Help Pay NYC's $4.2 Billion in Migrant Costs

Laura Nahmias
Wed, February 15, 2023 at 12:08 PM PST
(Bloomberg) -- New York Mayor Eric Adams pleaded with state lawmakers to help the city pay the estimated $4.2 billion in costs associated with providing care and shelter to more than 40,000 asylum-seeking migrants.
https://www.yahoo.com/finance/news/adams-begs-state-help-pay-200856189.html
Yes, just Remember the $COST$, of White Replacement! Yes, America will no longer be a White Majority nation, BUT it will most certainly be a POOR Third World Nation!

New York City Mayor Eric Adams

USA TODAY Opinion...(Invasion USA!) (Endless $Billions, just for White Replacement!)
Biden wants you to believe America's border crisis is getting better. Here's why it's not.
Chad Wolf
Thu, February 16, 2023 at 9:00 AM PST
"""""""The new plan the Biden administration announced in early January is designed to make the official border apprehension numbers decline, which will help create the mirage of a secure border. Specifically, DHS is now allowing 30,000 migrants per month into the country from Cuba, Haiti, Nicaragua and Venezuela through the use of the secretary's parole authority. Starting with January's apprehension numbers, these **30,000 per month, or 360,000 over the course of the year,** """""""
https://www.yahoo.com/news/biden-wants-believe-americas-border-100009704.html

[360,000?........That's 9 TIMES MORE invaders than Black New York City is complaining about FUNDING today! WHO is going to PAY, ALL those Endless $BILLIONS$ to take care of them?... YOU! Is the answer here! AFC]

Even Black cities, successfully Ethnically Cleansed of their White populations, have failed Malcolm X expectation's.

"We want, and must insist upon an area in this land that we can call our own, somewhere (where) we can hold our heads (up) with pride and dignity, without the continued harassments and indignities of our oppressors." Malcolm X.
BUT he never mentioned, or knew, that BLACK Oppression of Blacks can be/would be, even Worse than the 400 years of oppression by Whites, ever was!

Example.

Tyre Nichols death: Former Memphis police officers charged with second-degree murder
Last week, the five (Black) officers — Tadarrius Bean, Demetrius Haley, Emmitt Martin III, Desmond Mills Jr. and Justin Smith — involved in Nichols's Jan. 7 arrest were terminated.
Jayla Whitfield-Anderson·National Reporter
Thu, January 26, 2023 at 8:49 AM PST
https://www.yahoo.com/news/tyre-nichols-memphis-police-chief-warning-death-unrest-164908037.html
[BUT as it is Black on BLACK Crime and NOT a BLM Race WAR issue, the city will NOT Burn. AS Blacks, unlike Whites, will NOT allow Blacks to riot, loot and BURN Black cities with Impunity! AFC]

Revolt
Was white supremacy a driving force in the beating of Tyre Nichols by Black police officers?
Ashlee Banks
Mon, February 6, 2023 at 3:03 AM PST
https://www.yahoo.com/entertainment/white-supremacy-driving-force-beating-110316974.html

[Pathic! Really pathetic. Blacks BURN America to the ground with their 5,000 race riots, 250,000 Fires, to get their Civil Rights Laws that Ethnically Cleansed the cities of their White Populations, so they could live, "'THE DREAM" of Malcolm X.
 Blacks living FREE in an all Black City.
BUT then Blacks kept Acting Black, and the DEAD fill the city streets!
And still blacks BLAME their Murderous Actions on the 'Evil' White Man!
Pathic. AFC]

NOTE; [The (White) police are trying to maintain the First World America, that Most Americans enjoy. Democrats and Liberals want a more Third World America, with a more "'Relaxed" (Black) Third World policing system. As America continues to fall into the (Black) Third World, the More these White First World----Black Third World needs will collide.]

RACISM

A 'Racist' Or 'Racism', is a Religious violation, akin to being called a 'blasphemer'.
ONLY in Religion are the Races the same or 'Equal'. Thus a 'Racist' is just a person that sees the World and the People as they TRULY are and do Not follow the Religious beliefs of Political Correctness.
Blacks committed 5,000 race riots, 250,000 race riot fires, 1963-1973 to gain the Special civil rights powers and privileges they use against White America today, but that doesn't make them any nicer people.

Or even a Civilized people.

'Racism' is a silly word meant to Cover-up all the BLOOD and Terror that blacks commit!

Just Remember that Blacks commit MURDER/Violent Crime at a Rate that is 23 Times Higher than White People. "Racism?" Get REAL!

A 'Racist' is just a person that sees the World and the People as they TRULY are and do Not follow the Religious beliefs of Political Correctness.

Blacks committed 5,000 race riots, 250,000 race riot fires, 1963-1973 to gain the Special civil rights powers and privileges they use against White America today, but that doesn't make them any nicer people.
Or even a Civilized people.

Science has Proven Conclusively, 30 years ago, that the Races are Not the Same and Never can be 'Equal'.

Scientific proof of this would be the Kansas City Educational Experiment of the mid-1980s. Here a federal Judge Ordered the KCSD to raise the GPA of its black students. Years and $Billions later, after New buildings, new books, an Olympic sized swimming pool and even trips to Europe, for cultural enlightenment, there was no increase in black GPA. This was a nice CBS:60 Minutes program and all the results are a matter of Public record.
This was Humanities second most expensive and accurate scientific experiment, second only to the CERN of Europe, cost $many BILLIONS, took years to do and was inspected by third party inspectors to guarantee accuracy.

http://articles.chicagotribune.com/1995-06-22/news/9506220051_1_kansas-city-schools-performance-of-minority-students-national-norms

Chicago Tribune story from June 22, 1995 by Stephen Chapman titled AN EDUCATIONAL EXPERIMENT YIELDS SOME ASTONISHING SOBERING LESSONS Kansas City spent over $40K/yr per student in from 1985-

1995 and there was no measurable difference in (Black) test scores.

"The Supreme Court, which had approved the overhaul, now says the experiment can't go on forever. It rejected the school district's argument that state funds should keep flowing until student achievement rises to national norms."

"Until teachers and administrators are rewarded for success and punished for failure--like managers and employees in nearly every other American industry--the supply of failure will continue to exceed the demand. Kansas City has the best schools money can buy, but it has proven once and for all that good schools can't be bought."

https://www.cato.org/policy-analysis/money-school-performance-lessons-kansas-city-desegregation-experimen

Also, the terrible way that the World and Society Destroyed Nobel Prize Winning Scientist, Dr. James Watson, for his research on Race and IQ, shows that our Religious based 'Society' has not changed since the time of Copernicus.

BBC News… James Watson: Scientist loses titles after claims over race, 13 January 2019 Nobel Prize-winning American scientist James Watson has been stripped of his honorary titles after repeating comments about race and intelligence.

Dr. James Watson

WOKE is 100% Anti-White Man and is like Nazism in that it Blames ALL of a nation's problems on a Minority group, (White Men) so as to gain Special Powers for themselves while dodging any and all the Blame, for their own actions.

IF WOKE/CRT attacked JEWS instead of White Men it would be illegal!

PS:... Forcing people to believe in the Religion of WOKE, as a Term of Employment, is like Forcing the Jews to believe in Jesus as their Savior, as a term of Employment.

Example; Bank of America, Lowe's, and Truist Financial Corporation sponsored a woke Critical Race Theory program called "Racial Equity 21-Day Challenge" that was hosted by the United Way urging white individuals to "cede power to people of color."

August 20, 2021
Bank of America, Lowe's sponsor 'woke' training instructing white employees 'cede power to people of color' (bizpacreview.com)

A 38-page document is included in the training called "Awake to Woke to Work: Building a Race Equity Culture."
It contains a "Call to Action" which encourages white people to "cede power to people of color within and across teams, organizations, and systems." The document also advocates for participants to "decolonize your mind. Accept that White supremacy and institutional racism are real and practiced by all races." The document instructs readers to "dismantle" "White supremacy" and to call out "microaggressions."

"A generation of the unteachable is hanging upon us like a necklace of corpses."   **George Orwell**

"Diversity" is a sign in the window that says, "Help Wanted; White Men Need Not Apply".

Discrimination

Is but Freedom of Choice. It was this Freedom that separated Free men from Slaves as a Free man could choose whom he served and a Slave could not.

Now that the Religion of Race is backed up by the federal Government (for the last 60 + years). A Government that does not want to see its cities Burning, yet again, and its military in race Mutiny, Yet again. America is a de-fact-o Theology.

"In this country, intellectual cowardice is the worst enemy a writer or journalist has to face ... Unpopular ideas can be silenced, and inconvenient facts kept dark, without the need for any official ban ... At any given moment there is an orthodoxy, a body of ideas which it is assumed that all right-thinking people will accept without question." **George Orwell**

"Anyone who challenges the prevailing orthodoxy finds himself silenced with surprising effectiveness. A genuinely unfashionable opinion is almost never given a fair hearing." **~ George Orwell**

"The further a society drifts from the truth the more it will hate those that speak it." **George Orwell**

"The very concept of objective truth is fading out of the world. Lies will pass into history."
George Orwell

Affirmative Action

Yes, AA is just redistribution of Wealth, jobs, etc.

FROM those that lost the Race war, IE: Straight, White, Male, Protestants, TO the Winners, Blacks, Women, Jews, Homosexuals, Catholics, Muslims, etc.

Or as a famous person once said, "From those according to their Abilities, TO those according to their Needs."

And just like in the Old Soviet Union, 'business' is forced to hire people of the Governments choosing. Not the Best. Not those with the greatest potential of making the business successful, just the Governments chosen people.

That this government enforced policy destroys America's business and Industries is a given. Just as this policy destroyed the business and industries in the old Soviet Union.

PC is a Religion.

Political Correctness is a Religion, as it is a set of beliefs Not based on Science, Nor Reality. Yes, as the Religious Fanatics from the Politically Correct Religion suffer NO deviance from their beliefs. Attacking ALL that do not kneel to their faith.

I believe the Religion of Political Correctness was actually invented to cover up all those thousands and thousands of Black race riots. Otherwise, the very Legality of those Civil Rights laws would be put into open Question as Any 'law' passed under 'Duress', IE; the 'Threat of Violence' is illegal and unenforceable.

But PC has been expanded to mean all aspects of Government enforced 'Equality'. Even thou the Genders

and the Races, are Not the same, Not equal. It is an Oranges and Apples being 'Equal' fallacy.
Add this to this the Fact that the US Government is <u>Forbidden</u> from stuffing 'their' Religious beliefs down Americas throat by the First Amendment to the US Constitution and you will see Americas Dilemma. Enforce the Civil Rights Laws OR have Americas cities BURN AGAIN!

How the Democrats are Protecting the Legitimacy of the Civil Rights Laws.

[As a Point of Law, any 'law' passed under 'Duress', AKA; the 'Threat of Violence' is illegal and unenforceable.]

This is like the Legal concept that you Cannot inherit from your Grandmother IF it is known that you held a Gun to her head, so as to make yourself her sole beneficiary. BUT, IF no one knows you held a gun to your grandmother's head, as with the Liberals deleting all those thousands and thousands of Black race riots OUT of History, then it is OK. It is still illegal, but as long as this illegal Act is kept Secret, it is "The Law of the Land."
It is 'this' aspect (Note 2) of the law that forced the government to delete most all of these Race Riots, Fires and especially the Race Mutiny inside the US Military, that crippled Americas military and caused Americas loss in Vietnam with its 'Waste' of 58,002 American lives, 1.5 million Vietnamese lives, from US History books.

Few know, or want to know, that Liberals, Book Burned, US History, so as to make a Black President (obama) possible. Why do the Liberals get off Scott Free from illegally deleting thousands and thousands of Black race riots, 1963-

1973, Out of US History Books? Heck, most Americans do not even know that Blacks Burned 500 square blocks of Washington DC, 53 years ago, April, (1968). This deletion of history was not an accident. This was Intentional, for the easiest way to control the actions of another is to 'Control' the information these 'others' use in "Making their own Decisions". Thus, by controlling US History, (CRT, WOKE, Etc.) the Liberals Control the minds and actions of the American people, (As with Black Lives Matter, rioting, looting and burning of Americas cities) without the people of America ever knowing that they are being moved around like Puppets on a string.

"Orthodoxy **(PC)** is the ability to say two and two make five when faith requires it." **George Orwell**

In other words, **to protect the legitimacy of these Race Riot imposed, Civil Rights Laws, Liberals of high position and power (news media, Universities, government, etc.) have deleted, (Book Burned), most all of these events from America's memory, so as to cover-up their crimes against America.** As any 'law' passed under 'Duress', IE; the 'Threat of Violence' is illegal and unenforceable.

{It is 'this Secrecy', created and enforced by millions of people of Wealth and Power, for their own benefit, that I am exposing with this book.}

Unlike the Ray Bradbury book, "Fahrenheit 451" in which the Government must hunt down and Burn all the books that counter their NEW 'reality', today, in what we call the information age, the destruction/re-writing of information/history is just a click of the 'Delete' button away.

"Every record has been destroyed or falsified, every book rewritten, every picture has been repainted, every statue and street building has been renamed, every date has been altered. And the process is continuing day by day and minute by minute. History has stopped. Nothing exists except an endless present in which the Party is always right." 1984,
George Orwell

Why? You might ask did the US Government delete all this information. Simple, the Civil Rights Laws were/are *wildly popular* **with the vast majority of Americans.**
The previously mentioned 78% of America. AKA: Civil Rights Coalition members, Women, Blacks, Jews, Catholics, etc.

And IF it were not for the US Supreme Court's Decision on, Row vs Wade, (1972) that legalized a Women's 'Right' to an abortion, (that also split the Women's Vote), I feel that America today, would be a One-Party State. As there would not be enough Republican votes to elect a person as Dogcatcher.

The most effective way to destroy people is to deny and obliterate their own understanding of their history.
<u>George Orwell</u>

''**This is a real revolution. Revolution is always based on land. Revolution is never based on begging somebody for an integrated cup of coffee. Revolutions are never fought by turning the other cheek. Revolutions are never based upon love your enemy and pray for those who spitefully use you. And revolutions are never waged singing "We Shall**

Overcome." Revolutions are based upon bloodshed. Revolutions are never compromising. Revolutions are never based upon negotiations. Revolutions are never based upon any kind of tokenism whatsoever...

Revolutions overturn systems, and there is no system on this earth which has proven itself more corrupt, more criminal, than this system that in 1964 still colonizes twenty-two million African -Americans''.   Malcolm X New York, April 8, 1964

'The Black revolution is the struggle of the non-whites of this Earth against their white oppressors.

The Black revolution has swept white supremacy out of Africa, out of Asia, and is getting ready to sweep it out of Latin America.

Revolutions are based on land. Revolutionaries are the landless against the landlord.

Revolutions are never peaceful, never loving, never nonviolent.

Nor are they ever compromising. Revolutions are destructive and bloody.

Revolutionaries don't compromise with the enemy; they don't even negotiate. Like the flood in Noah's day, revolution drowns all opposition, or like the fire in Lot's day, the Black revolution burns everything that gets in its path.'

Malcolm X

New York, April 8, 1964. Minister of the Nation of Islam. AKA; The Black Muslims

Blacks 'won' their war against the White US Government. Destroyed Americas freedoms and gave themselves vast powers over America.

Blacks, a 12% minority, acquired their Vast Powers over America by the 'liberal' use of Violence and Terrorism.

"No advance in wealth, no softening of manners, no reform or revolution has ever brought human equality a millimeter nearer." — **George Orwell**

WHITE PRIVILEGE

Is like when the French Cafe owners of 1943 Paris preferred to serve their French Customers instead of the Germans.
Blacks committed 5,000 race riots, 250,000 race riot fires, 1963-1973 to gain the Special civil rights powers and privileges they use against White America today, but that doesn't make them any nicer people.

Or, maybe 'White Privilege', as in Not having a Prison Record? As in Not Burning Americas cities in the name of 'Justice', etc.
Just because Blacks 'Won' their race war against White America, does not make them any more 'Civilized' as a People.

Yes, there just might be another 'Reason' for this so-called 'White Privilege'. This being FEAR of 'Normal Black behavior'.

Note: [Since the end of the draft in 1973 the U.S. military has succeeded in whitening the combat arms by excluding low test scorers, high school dropouts, and people with criminal records--a huge chunk of African American youth. (Twelve percent of Black males in their 20s and early 30s are in jail or prison on any given day.)]

Buffalo soldiers: Glen Ford examines the U.S. military's track record of racial hostilities. (Enemies of the State). - Free Online Library (thefreelibrary.com)

Malcolm X, the true leader of the Civil Rights Movement.
"If it's necessary to form a Black Nationalist army, we'll form a Black nationalist army. It'll be the ballot or the bullet. It'll be liberty or it'll be death!"
     Malcolm X, April 1964

Here is 'why' President Kennedy (Catholic) supported the Jewish-written Civil Rights Act of 1964.

Nov 8, 1960 Kennedy Defeats Nixon in 1960 Election

John F. Kennedy is elected the 35th President of the United States, defeating his Republican opponent, Richard Nixon, by a slim margin of only 118,000 votes nationwide.

April 17, 1961   Bay of Pigs

Less than three months into JFK's presidency, a group of CIA-trained Cuban exiles attempts to invade Cuba at the Bay of Pigs. The Cuban army quickly thwarts their efforts, and the Kennedy-approved fiasco becomes a major embarrassment for the new president.

Oct. 6, 1961, JFK urges Americans to build bomb shelters.

President John F. Kennedy, speaking on Civil defense, advises American families to build bomb shelters to protect them from atomic fallout in the event of a nuclear exchange with the Soviet Union. Kennedy also assured the public that the U.S. Civil defense program would soon begin providing such protection for every American. Only one year later, true to Kennedy's fears, the world hovered on the brink of full-scale nuclear war when the Cuban Missile Crisis erupted over the USSR's placement of nuclear missiles in Cuba. During the tense 13-day crisis, some Americans prepared for nuclear war by buying up canned goods and completing last-minute work on their backyard bomb shelters.

Cuban Missile Crisis, Oct 16, 1962

JFK is shown photos of Soviet nuclear missile sites being installed in Cuba. To minimize Soviet power in the West, the president initiates a blockade of Cuba the following week. For nearly two weeks, the Cuban Missile Crisis will bring the world closer to nuclear war than ever before or after.

Now enters Dr. Martin Luther King Jr's/Malcolm X, Race/Religious War against White America, just as President Kennedy puts <u>all the World on the very edge of Nuclear Annihilation.</u> As mentioned at the beginning of this book.

It was a time when the fate of the World balanced on the edge of a <u>radioactive knife</u>.
It was a time when one wrong move, one wrong word, <u>could end all Humankind</u>.

It was at this 'perfect moment in history', when the enemy of the Black Race was <u>deadly vulnerable,</u> that the indomitable spirit of Malcolm X arose from the ghetto.

His passionate words of POWER, FIRE, WEALTH and FREEDOM from White Man's Rule, inspired Americas most <u>devastating Race War</u>.

This Jihad this was so powerful, so bloody, so destructive, so successful, so utterly terrifying in every way to White America, that it is <u>not spoken of</u> for fear of starting, it all over again!   AFC

I, personally use, as the start of those 5,000 modern Civil Rights Movements race riots, with the MLK lead Race Riot, in Birmingham AL, 1963.

From April 3 to May 12, 1963 Martin Luther King Jr. personally lead a 6 weeklong siege of Birmingham AL, called "Project C". It was in hopes of getting the White police to use Violence against the Black children, in front of all those TV cameras, also known as a PR Stunt. King gets his wish, [Whites responded with two small bombs] and his reward was a massive Black Race riot that did more to force JFK's hand on Civil Rights Law, than all the Police Dogs and fire hoses in Birmingham. The race riot was so terrible as to shock all of America with its level of violence. Two other 'support' race riots, in other cities, also ensued as a sign of Black solidarity.

JFK was so terrified of what the USSR would do with a Black uprising across all of America, crippling America, and worse, crippling Americas, now DE-segregated Military. All this, less than seven (7) months after all of Humanity was almost ended, during the Cuban Missile Crisis.

JFK gave to Congress the Civil Rights Act of 1964 within 38 days of Kings, Birmingham race riot.

Note: [The Civil Rights Act of 1964 and the Voting Rights Act of 1965 were drafted in the conference room of Religious Action Center of Reform Judaism]

https://rac.org/jews-and-Civil-Rights-movement

The Civil Rights Laws/Act of 1964, fundamentally changed the 'power structure' of America. These Laws were passed to stop America from being burned to the ground. And maybe nuked to oblivion by a USSR that saw a weak America in the throes of a Race War. A Civil War.

President John F. Kennedy (JFK) also had a nationally televised speech to the nation on Civil Rights, June 11, 1963 in which he mentioned mass <u>Black Violence 12 times</u> and called the Civil Rights Movement a 'Revolution'.

https://genius.com/John-f-kennedy-civil-rights-address-june-11-1963-annotated

With JFKs UN-intended encouragement, Blacks/CRM members continued with thousands of race riots over the coming years. And unto today and no doubt, tomorrow.

JFK Assassinated, November 22, 1963.

{Fun note.} In my neighborhood, it was rumored that JFK was assassinated by the MOB, because he had Welshed on $30 million, he had borrowed from the MOB in order to run for the Presidency in 1960.
And it is <u>'this' embarrassment</u>, that has kept JFK's assassination, "Unresolved'' for all these decades.

For those people that said/say that Dr. Martin Luther King Jr. was a ''Man-of-Peace'' I will say that they never saw King's BURNING of Birmingham AL, 1963.
Ethnic Cleansing of Birmingham AL, Population by race.

Year	Total	Black%	White%
1960	340,887	39.6%	60.3%
2010	212,237	73.4%	22.3%

Civil Rights Act of 1964
Americas Left Turn to Marxist Rule.

From Wikipedia, the free encyclopedia
The legislation had been proposed by President John F. Kennedy in June 1963, but it was opposed by filibuster in the Senate. After Kennedy was assassinated on November 22, 1963, President Lyndon B. Johnson pushed the bill forward. The United States House of Representatives passed the bill on February 10, 1964, and after a 54-day filibuster, it passed the United States Senate on June 19, 1964. The final vote was 290–130 in the House of Representatives and 73–27 in the Senate.[6] After the House agreed to a subsequent Senate amendment, the

Civil Rights Act was signed into law by President Johnson at the White House on July 2, 1964.
The act "remains one of the most significant legislative achievements in American history".[5]

Historical/Religious NOTE:

The Civil Rights Act of 1964 and the Voting Rights Act of 1965 were drafted in the conference room of Religious Action Center of Reform Judaism, under the aegis of the Leadership Conference which for decades was located in the RAC's building.

https://rac.org/issues/civil-rights-voting-rights/brief-history-jews-and-civil-rights-movement-1960s

Personal Note; "This law caused the greatest destruction of Freedom; America has ever endured."
OR call it, "Americas Great Left Turn", if you prefer.

Note; Blacks/CRMC did what the Confederates, Nazi Germany or the entire Empire of Japan failed to accomplish. To bring down the US Government, burn its cities, conquer America to its 'Soul', destroy Americas Freedoms and form a New Society in their own image.

FUN NOTE: When those "liberals" used those 5,000 black race riots, 1963-1973, to bring the US Government to its knees and install a 'New' society, in their own image, just as Hitler did in Europe, they became fascist and so did the government, as the US Government and all its vassal state/etc. governments, needed fascist powers to enforce those civil rights laws.

Note; "Unlike socialism, fascism is not opposed to private ownership of capital, provided that business owners are co-operative and do not resist state control".

It is actually funny, in a very dark way, here President Johnson (LBJ) would be/was, killing MILLIONS of Vietnamese AND tens of thousands of Americans, in the name of stopping Marxist ideology in Vietnam, while imposing Marxist style, government control of everything and everyone right here in America in the name of "Civil Rights."

Not that 'he' was given much of a choice.
Here are a few of the many, many riots of 1964, as an example of what those 10 years were like.

PS: LBJ signed the Civil Rights Act of 1964 into law, on July 2 1964 after many months of very few race riots.

1. New York City–July 18-23–1 killed–144 injured–519 arrested– 541 stores damaged!
2. Rochester–July 24-25–4 killed–350 injured– 976 arrested–204 stores damaged.
3. Jersey City–August 2-4--46 injured–52 arrested– 71 stores damaged.
4. Paterson–August 11-13–8 injured–65 arrested–20 stores damaged.
5. Elizabeth–August 11-13–6 injured–18 arrested–17 stores damaged.
6. Chicago (Dixmoor) August 16-17–57 injured–80 arrested–2 stores damaged.
7. Philadelphia–August 28-30– 341 injured–774 arrested– 225 stores damaged.

"The point is that we are all capable of believing things which we know to be untrue, and then, when we are finally proved wrong, impudently twisting the facts so as to show that we were right. Intellectually, it is possible to carry on this process for an indefinite time: the only check on it is that sooner or later a false belief bumps up against solid reality, usually on a battlefield."   **George Orwell**

CIA Report:

August 28, 1967

Date declassified: September 20, 1979

Microfiche: 1980 Document #238ACentral Intelligence Agency. "_____ comments on the affect of food shortages, bombing raids and the American race riots on North Vietnamese morale." 1967.

"North Vietnamese morale has been boosted considerably by the Civil Rights and the 'Black Power' movement in the United States. The North Vietnam government has indicated to the French Mission in Hanoi that the riots and the emergence of the 'Black Power' movement, signal the beginning of a popular revolution in the United States against the ruling classes. The North Vietnamese government also believes that the Civil Rights disturbances will adversely affect American participation in the Vietnam War. The United States government will be forced to divert large sums of money to educational, housing, and other social reforms to maintain the loyalty of the underprivileged elements and prevent them from joining the ranks of the Civil Rights dissidents. The North Vietnamese further believe that the United States will have to maintain more troops in the United States to control the rioters." End

This last prediction proved to be true more than the CIA would have ever cared to imagine. The late 1960s and early 1970s saw a tremendous rise in racial conflict on bases both in the United States and Vietnam.

Here is a small sample, in more detail, of what those 10 years of Race Rebellion were like. All of it would fill libraries with their Flaming Chaos!

THE 1967 DETROIT REBELLION

Revolutionary worker #915, July 13, 1997

July 1997 marks the 30th anniversary of one of the most powerful uprisings of the 1960's—an urban rebellion in Detroit which shook the rulers of this Country as never before.

In the summer of 1967, a news magazine had selected Detroit to be an August cover story for having the "best race relations in North America."

Detroit Mayor Jerome Cavanagh was a "progressive urban leader." He was proud of all he had done for "his city." He had appointed several Black people to key posts. He administered a full range of anti-poverty programs, summer employment efforts, and activities at recreation center. An Early Warning System had just been instituted to "feel the pulse of the inner city." It was a network of thousands of informants among the police officers, poverty workers, parks employees, and others in daily contact with the ghetto who phoned in tips about racial tension. Finally, just to make sure, the mayor's Summer Task Force began a "riot simulation" on July 20. Leaders of the police and fire departments, the Civil Rights Commission, and various other city agencies discussed how they would respond to a civil disturbance. They chose a random location at Twelfth Street and Clairmount Avenue.

Three days later in the early morning hours of July 23, Twelfth and Clairmount erupted. The cover story of Newsweek expressed the panic of the power structure.

"The trouble burst on Detroit like a firestorm and turned the nation's fifth biggest city into a theater of war. Whole streets lay ravaged by looters, whole blocks immolated by flames. (black flames) Federal troops – the first sent into racial battle outside the South in a quarter of a century – occupied American Streets at bayonet point.

Patton tanks, machine guns ablaze – and Huey helicopters patrolled a city-scape of blackened brick chimneys poking out of gutted basements.

And suddenly Harlem 1964 and Watts 1965 and Newark only three weeks ago fell into the shadows of memory.

Detroit was the new benchmark, its rubble a monument to the most devastating race riot in U.S. history – and a symbol of domestic crisis grown graver than any since the Civil War.

"The club! Those godamn pecker woods are going to raid the club again!"

A rowdy crowd of about 200 gathering at 3:30 a.m. Sunday beside a police paddy wagon that has just pulled up across from the United Community League for Civic Action, on Twelfth near Clairmount.

Originally a Black activist club, the UCLCA was a target of the white political machine. When the club owner was laid off from his job in the auto plants, he started using it as a "blind pig" – an after-hours drinking and gambling joint – in order to survive. The routine police raids normally netted about 20 people, just enough to cram into a single paddy wagon.

But tonight, unknown to the cops, there is a party going on for two Black GI'S just home from Vietnam. Inside, 85 people celebrate their safe return.

One of the cops swings a sledgehammer through the plate glass door to get in. Cursed volley back and forth between the crowd and the police. "Go home whitey. Why don't you go fuck with white people?"

Club patrons are being hustled into a paddy wagon, their arms twisted painfully behind their backs. With each wagon load, the crowd grows larger and more angry. Soon, some of the onlookers, outraged at how roughly the women are being arrested, are yelling at the top of their lungs. The cops line up in the middle of the street with their batons ready. "If you stay where you are, no one will get hurt."

But Bill Scott 19-year-old son of the club owner, climbs on top of a care. "Are we going to let these peckerwood mother fuckers come down here any time they want and mess us around?" Hell, no! Barks the crowd.

As the paddy wagon and cop cars pull away, a hail of bricks and bottles smashes against them.

Against background of burglar alarms and laugher, a stunned cop yells into his radio receiver, "all cars stay clear. Repeat. Stay clear of Twelfth Street area."

(This scenario is drawn in large part from Hurt, Baby, Hurt, by William Walter Scott.)

The Kerner Commission Report noted that "Late Sunday afternoon it appeared to one observer that the young people were **'dancing amidst the flames.'**"

Bill Scott would later set down on paper the elation he felt when the people seized control of Twelfth Street:

"I felt powerful and good inside for being a part of those who finally fought back regardless of fear – Within the aggregation of people this night there was a certain unique madness that had taken possession of everyone's body and soul which was almost what could be called the unification of the rebellious spirit of man; a fearless spirit ordained for complete liberation of the self, combined with and supported by a community at large. Guess one could say it was like fighting an gaining your citizenship, after having given it away to obedience to the law –police law– which was one-man judge and assassin that ruled Black people"

(Hurt Baby, Hurt) The police sergeant who led the raid on the "blind pig" recalls;

"The real trouble didn't start until we started to leave with the last wagon load, and we couldn't get our cars out. By the time we pulled away, more bottles and bricks were coming. A lot of the windows were broken out in one of the cars. We answered radio runs for looting, fire, shooting, curfew violations and anything else that happened.

"The sniping was real. I was in the station more than once when we were being sniped at the desk in the station. Some of the motormen tell me that in the armored personnel carriers, you'd hear a bang or a ping on the outside, and you couldn't tell for sure if somebody had thrown a rock or if somebody shot at you.

"Yes I was scared. You're damned right I was scared. More than once I was scared." (Excerpts from an oral history by Sidney Fine.)

Keeping the Black people of Detroit "in line" was the task of the city police force, which was 93 percent white. Neighborhoods were prowled by the Big Four, the police cruisers whose four officers would "beat the hell out of you for recreation."

In late June 1967 Danny Thomas, a Black 27-year-old army vet who lived only four blocks from Twelfth and Clairmount, was killed by a gang of white youths when he tried to protect his pregnant wife from their sexual advances. She later lost the baby. The police refused to arrest the gang. The incident was kept out of the major newspapers until city's Black newspaper made it a banner headline.

Detroit typified a situation where Black people were right at the heart of American society as urban workers, and, at the same time, forcibly held in an exploited and oppressed condition relative to whites Detroit was Motor City. And in the auto plants, discrimination was deep, and the United Auto Workers (UAW) – which had excluded Black members for years – was blatantly racist. In the Twelfth Street area about 30 percent of Blacks under 25 were unemployed and population density in the rundown apartments was 21,000 persons per square mile-double the city average.

A sense of anger simmering in places like Twelfth Street is expressed by Bill Scott, when he recalls how he felt after weeks of searching for a job in the summer of 1967:

"(One) day I realized with complete understanding that something was wrong because there should have been a job for me somewhere in that entire city... I had just finished submitting a job application at one of the many downtown employment officers and was on my way back to my sister's home, when something came to me like the ring of a bell which caused me to ask myself one question, "Tell me something, Billy, why is it that you don't see any of these white cats walking around looking for a job, not to mention that they are on their lunch breaks, well-dressed, and carefree as anybody would want to be?" This was the day I decided to reject anything that was white. I could no longer tell myself that it was going to work out... There was nothing in the white world that had been meant for me...nothing. I wasn't even supposed to be out there in the first place. And going to college wasn't going to change the way white people mistreated and murdered Black people in any way possible." (Hurt, Baby, Hurt)

July 23, 1967

"That Sunday, my wife went to church on Twelfth Street, not to far from where the incident had occurred. And she came back, she said you know, there's a sort of stillness that's there that I don't understand. She said it's to calm. And I said, well, you know, there is something rather strange. And we looked outside and there was an inordinate amount of fires (black fires) that were trickling up through the air!"

This recollection on the tense calm that settled into the initial six-block riot area during the first daylight hours after the police retreat comes from a Black teacher. About 25 years old at the time of the rebellion, he worked evenings as a driver and was able to observe much of the rebellion over the next few days. But on Sunday, city officials, caught off-guard– their forces vastly outnumbered in the initial outbreak– were hoping the disturbance would ebb by itself through a policy of police restraint and media blackout. He continues:

"The mayor, Jerome P. Cavanagh, said don't shoot the looters. I think part of the reason why that was the case, they said that was that the Black community had been responsible for his being elected. Well what started, I would say for the next two days, or so, a sort of interracial stealing binge, in which you had Black folks and white folks hand-in-hand going into various stores, pillaging them, giving a certain amount of time for the people to get their goods, and then they would flee the area."

In a picnic-like atmosphere of tinkling glass, shouts of laughter, and Motown music blaring from transistor radios, for two days the way wealth flowed in the city was reversed on a grand scale. Impoverished folk liberated basic foodstuffs from grocery stores where they'd been cheated for years, and less-needy residents could be seen rolling sofas out of exclusive stores like Charles Furniture on Olympia Street. The owner of a music shop reported losing every electric guitar, amplifier, and jazz album in the place– but the classical records were left untouched.

The burning and looting were seen as one way to strike back at the discrimination, the hidden "ghetto taxes" and how all of life was stacked against Black people in America. One auto worker, who stayed away form his job at a Ford plant on Monday told a reporter:

"People are bitter. White people gyp you all the time. I went to a gas station at Wyandotte and Michigan to get at tire changed. It was raining and the man wouldn't change it. Then he wanted to charge me $12 to change it because I'm a Negro. That kind of stuff is wrong. I've been looking for this riot to happen for years."

As he escorted the reporter on a tour of the looted area, he stopped in front of a now- empty furniture store:

"You go in there to buy furniture and those people would act like they were doing you a favor. They send furniture down here that the white people wouldn't have and then they charge you double for it. It's too much."

Late that evening, a 45-year-old white man in a grocery-looting team of whites and black was shot to death by a market owner. It was the first fatality in the riot. Five different banks were stormed, all to no avail. But among the more prized items taken were total of 2,498 rifles and 38 handguns.

The role of ghetto youth in all stages of the rebellion stood out clearly.

Youngsters who have been routinely brutalized by the cops could hardly believe their own sudden strength.

This was not lost on city officials who grimly concluded afterwards that 60 percent of those participating had been between 15 and 24 years old. In the aftermath of the rebellion Mayor Cavanagh showed movies of the rebellion to the members of the Kerner Commission in Washington:

"Look at the faces. You will see mostly young men. These young men are the fuse. For the most part they have no experience in real productive work. For the most part, they have no stake in the social arrangements of life. For the most part, they have no foreseeable future except among the hustlers and minor racketeers.

For the most part, they are cynical, hostile, frustrated, and angry against a system they feel has included them out. At the same time, they are filled with the bravado of youth and a code of behavior which is hostile to authority" (John Hersey, The Algiers Motel Incident.)

A 9-5 curfew imposed. But the city police were no match for the huge and youthful mobs, and Cavanagh was forced to call in 350 state troopers and 900 Michigan National Guardsmen on the very first day of the rebellion. The guardsmen were summoned from their summer encampment in a rural area of the state. Many had never visited a large city nor seen a Black person except on television. When their convoy reached Grand Blanc and they saw an ominous plume of smoke rising above the unseen city 45 miles further to the southeast- they were issued ammunition.

Undisciplined, trigger-happy,(typical, timeless, whitey) without any riot training other than a few words about "mob control," the guardsmen were dispatched from various high school staging areas down the darkened city streets. By Monday there were 800 state police and over 9,000 guardsmen in the city-85 percent of all Guard forces statewide.

According to various accounts, it was sometime on Monday that the character of the rebellion went through a change. Gunfire against the authorities, which had started the preceding evening, became the favored activity of the rioters, both Black and white. It began with Fire Department personnel drawing hostile bullets. All told, on 285 occasions firemen had to retreat from the scene of a fire. When armed officers intervened, fierce gun battles erupted between the rebels and the police and National Guardsmen. It was reported that during a single hour on Monday, for example, a police dispatcher counted two precinct stations, two riot command posts, and five stations all under sniper fire.

On Monday afternoon, President Johnson dispatch a task force of 4,750 paratroopers of the 82nd and 101st Airborne Divisions, from Ft. Bragg and Ft. Campbell to Selfridge of Air Force Base north of Detroit. He also sent a team of personal envoys, headed by Cyrus Vance (former Deputy Secretary of Defense under Kennedy and later Secretary of State under Carter.) But there was deep division within ruling circles over the deployment of these troops, which had been requested 12 hours earlier by Governor Romney and Mayor Cavanagh.

Finally, Johnson authorized that the federal troops be deployed and, simultaneously, that the Guard be federalized. With the guardsmen already stationed on the west side where the rebellion had erupted, the army soldiers were deployed on the east side, where the rebellion had only recently spread. Thus, on Tuesday, some of the rebels moved away from the crack federal troops and shifted over to the west side of the city. Gun-fighting continued for another two or three days.

The Detroit News described the scene in the Wednesday edition:

"Negro snipers turned 140 square blocks north of West Garand Blvd. Into a bloody battlefield for three hours last night, temporarily routing police and national guardsmen... Tanks thundered through the streets and heavy machine guns clattered. The scene was incredible. It was as though the Viet Cong had infiltrated the riot-blackened streets."

Some observers perceived a certain degree of organization among the rioters. Whatever degree of organization that people had built expressed itself powerfully in various ways. The role of Vietnam veterans stood out in the rebellion. Those who had been sent to fight for U.S. imperialism in the rice paddies and jungles of Vietnam were turning the guns around. The war had come home. One observer testified that he'd overheard an early walkie-talkie command to spread the disorder to the east side. The authorities in their command centers saw things everywhere-some real, some not. The Fire Chief believed that arsonists used divide-and-conquer tactics and that other lured his men into gun ambushes by telephoning bogus reports of fires. A survey of metro-area residents two weeks after the rebellion found that 55.5 percent thought it had been planned, and many were inclined to call it an insurrection or revolution.

The sheer scale of this rebellion was impressive. Consider the portion of the city which police designated the "central civil disorder area. "This area alone straddled both sides of the city, extending over 40 of the city's 140 square miles (over 350 square kilometers). When the smoke finally cleared, some 1,300 buildings had been burned and 2,700 looted, property damage exceeded $50 million, and 5,000 people were left homeless by wind-swept fires. There were 7, 231 arrested (6,407 of them Black), 386 injured, and 43 dead. Thirty-three of those killed in the rebellion were Black.

In addition, the rebellion ignited similar uprisings, all of them serious enough to deploy National Guardsmen or state police– in five other cities: Pontiac, Flint, and Saginaw to the north: Grand Rapids, some 150 miles to the west: and

Toledo, Ohio to the south. Disturbances of varying intensity were also simultaneously occurring in more than two dozen cities in Michigan, Ohio and other states.

After surveying the rubble, Henry Ford II, chairman of Ford Motor Company, was asked to comment.

"It is my feeling that this country may turn out to be the laughing stock of the world because of situations such as we've had in Detroit. I don't think there is much point in trying to sell the world on emulating our system and way of life if we can't even put our own house in order." (Automotive News)

The ruling class was deeply disturbed: this uprising in one of the chief industrial centers of the nation's heartland, quelled only by the intervention of the U.S. Army, had broadcast a message to the whole world that the American system was bankrupt—and vulnerable.

A single week of rebellion allows the oppressed to distinguish friends better than whole years of normal times.

Early on the first day of the rebellion, Hubert Locke, a Black administrative assistant to Detroit's police commissioner, called together several of the city's Responsible Negro Leaders. In pairs, they fanned out through the tenth Precinct to plead with the crowds to disperse. One pair comprised Deputy School Superintendent Arthur Johnson and U.S. Representative John Conyers, Jr., who was quite popular among his constituents.

At one intersection, Conyers stood on the hood of the car and shouted through a bullhorn, "We're with you! But, Please! This is not the way to do things! Please go back to your homes!" "No, no, no," the crowd chanted, "Don't want to hear it!" "Uncle Tom!" One man in the crowd, a civil rights activist whom Conyers had once defended in a trail, was inciting the crowd and shouting at Conyers, "Why are you defending the cops and the establishment?

You're just as bad as they are! "Rocks and bottles flew toward the car, one of them hitting a cop nearby. The crowd was getting "uglier." Johnson whispered into Conyers' ear, "John, let's get the hell out of here." As Conyers climbed down form the hood of the car, he remarked to reporter in disgust, "You try to talk to those people and they'll knock you into the middle of next year."

The RW asked D., a Black revolutionary who was very young at the time, how much the rebellion of the "young kids" had impinged on the routine of the older Black workers, like his father. He recalled:

"At home that's all they talked about. Even with a lot of the older Blacks, there was mixed feeling. You had a lot of them, they finally sensed that this is the beginning of something: finally the Black folks rose up. A lot of that hostility and outrage toward the system is coming out, it was being actualized in Black youth. From just the young brother and sister throwing a rock through a window and grabbing something, or a old person just hollering – it affected everybody."

One of the most distinctive aspects of the Detroit rebellion, even compared to other urban rebellions of the decade, was the mass participation of the working class, including basic industrial workers. The rebellion was a sort of "weather vane" that pointed to the revolutionary potential of the urban proletariat, and it was a reference point for a revolutionary movement that grew in the auto plants during the next few years.

Participation in the rebellion was highest among the most deprived strata of the black working class, but it also extended broadly to Blacks and whites of various strata. In Detroit, people who could be classified "lower middle class" rioted side-by-side with those on the bottom of society. A survey of 1,200 men being held at Jackson prison after their arrest in the rebellion found that 40 percent were employed by the Big 3 auto companies, and an additional 40 percent by other large, mostly unionized employers. Also 80 percent received wages of at least $6,000 (in 1967 dollars), which was only slightly below the citywide family income average at the time–which was $6,400 for Blacks and $6,800 for whites. (Poverty level was $3,335 for an urban family of four.)

In the auto plants themselves, absenteeism was so high during the rebellion that many assembly operations ground to a halt for two days. The afternoon and evening shifts were cancelled due to the curfew, even though the curfew was not enforced against person commuting to and from work. But even on the day shift, with no curfew in effect, many plants in both Detroit and Pontiac experienced absenteeism levels as high as 80 to 85 percent.

While large numbers of auto workers were in the thick of the rebellion, within the auto plants them-selves, the atmosphere, although tense did not erupt into violence or walkouts as the companies feared. The Automotive News commented, "the automotive industry almost miraculously escaped the fury."

But the rebellion upped the ante in the already racially polarized factories. One worker, who commuted from the black suburb of Inkster to work in Detroit, recalled for the

RW the atmosphere inside one of the Big 3. During the week of the rebellion, some white foremen locked themselves in the foremen's office at shift-end until all the Black workers had left, afraid that they might get hurt. In the immediate wake of the rebellion, workers who had involved were circumspect about their activities. "They didn't talk much about it. Some stole more than the kids. "Nevertheless, due to the liberated climate overall, the political balance had shifted on the factory floors. For example, previously" you had Black Uncle Toms who didn't want to sit with Blacks. But when the riots happened they left the whites and came to sit with the Blacks. I told them, "Go back where you came from."

There are some lessons learned young which stubbornly linger. Twenty years after the rebellion, one who was ten years old in 1967 had this to say:

"What is showed, actually, is that revolution is possible in the United States. Looking back, that it's possible. The fact that the riots had a significant impact on everybody, not only Blacks but Chicanos, Puerto Ricans, Native Americans, and even the progressive whites, it had radicalized everybody. Not only that, it had an impact on people all over the world, that something like this could take place right here in the United States. Before 1967, Blacks thought it was impossible to really rise up against the system that way. And it showed, too, the potentialities of the masses of Blacks, if the energies and hostilities are directed at the oppressor. That's how I look back on '67.' It's been so much written about it, it's so much to actually learn about it and consciously relearn about the '60's. But really it symbolized revolution is ripe and can happen right here in the citadel of imperialism." END

''This is a real revolution. Revolution is always based on land. Revolution is never based on begging somebody for an integrated cup of coffee. Revolutions are never fought by turning the other cheek. Revolutions are never based upon love your enemy and pray for those who spitefully use you. And revolutions are never waged singing "We Shall Overcome." Revolutions are based upon bloodshed. Revolutions are never compromising. Revolutions are never based upon negotiations. Revolutions are never based upon any kind of tokenism whatsoever...
Revolutions overturn systems, and there is no system on this earth which has proven itself more corrupt, more criminal, than this system that in 1964 still colonizes twenty-two

million African-Americans''.   Malcolm X   New York, April 8, 1964

Today the Race Rebellion continues. As so too does the Ethnic Cleansing of America's cities.

The George Floyd Race Riots.

A little history here I think. As the WAR between Black Criminals/BLM Terrorists and the Police has been going on for very many years.

On July 7, 2016, Micah Xavier Johnson (Black, BLM) ambushed a group of White police officers in Dallas, Texas, shooting and killing five White officers and injuring nine others. Two civilians were also wounded. Johnson was an Army Reserve Afghan War veteran and was angry over police shootings of black men. The shooting happened at the end of a protest against the police killings of Alton Sterling in Baton Rouge, Louisiana, and Philando Castile in Falcon Heights, Minnesota, which had occurred in the preceding days.

The murder by that BLM sniper, of the those 5 White police officers in Dallas came a day after an obama speech in which he stated (without a shred of evidence to back it up) that "racist cops were killing black folks for no reason". Did obama indirectly ORDER the Murders of those 5 White Policeman in Dallas?

NOTE: White People did NOT riot, loot, and BURN any Black Cities over this mass Murder of White Police officers by a Black, (BLM) Black Lives Matter Member. THIS more than anything shows the Vast difference between the Black Culture and the White Culture.

GEORGE FLOYD

Published May 31, 2020 11:11pm EDT
George Floyd unrest: Riots, fires, violence escalate in several major cities

Chaos broke out in several major U.S. cities on Sunday night as rioters hijacked what had been peaceful protests over the death of **George Floyd** in Minneapolis police custody.

Among the turmoil: Fires lit near the White House, including at St. John's Church just a short walk away; rioters clashing with police in New York City; and the Los Angeles County sheriff saying people still out on the streets were "acting like terrorists."

The **National Guard's top general** on Sunday said Guard units in nearly half of U.S. states have been mobilized to help major cities deal with the riots. Gen. Joseph Lengyel said some 16,000 additional Guard troops have been deployed to 24 states and the **District of Columbia** in response to civil disturbances.

Floyd died Monday after a Derek Chauvin, a white Minneapolis police officer, pressed his knee on Floyd's neck. The officer has been charged with third-degree murder and second-degree manslaughter; he and three other officers were fired from the force after video of Floyd's death emerged.

Police Officer Derek Chauvin

https://www.foxnews.com/us/george-floyd-cities-brace-riots-national-guard-troops-mobilize

---

U.S.INSIDER
Hundreds of officers quit the Minneapolis police department after George Floyd was killed. The department is reportedly still struggling to recruit.
https://www.yahoo.com/news/hundreds-officers-quit-minneapolis-police-135604068.html

"George Floyd" was a career Criminal that died while Resisting Arrest. Criminals, Terrorists, Black Supremist, being Bored with the COVID lockups, used THIS as an excuse Continue the Race WAR upon the 'Evil' White Man, and to Have some FUN and Riot, and Loot and BURN some cities! It goes without saying that IF.....
If Floyd had been White, No cities would have been Burned.

IF the Policeman had been Black, NO Cities would have been Burned.
That the Government threw the Police to the Black Mobs says much.
That 50,000 White people have already fled the city of Minneapolis also says that the Ethnic Cleansing of Americas cities is continuing.
That Minneapolis is a Dying city, is obvious.

[Proof of my statements would be the Very obviousness. As in NO Burning Cities, when those 5 Black Memphis Policemen beat to death a Black man they stopped for a traffic violation.]

One Example from today, but was a copy of those millions of times over the decades, as the cities BURNED and FRAR filled the streets;

"I've lived in Minneapolis my entire life. I'm leaving Friday. I no longer recognize my hometown."

GRACE BUREAU - GUSTAVUS ADOLPHUS COLLEGE •APRIL 22, 2021
SHARE THIS ARTICLE: The College Fix on Facebook The College Fix on Twitter The College Fix on Reddit Share on Email

OPINION: *I no longer recognize Minneapolis. I no longer want to live here.*
MINNEAPOLIS, Minn. — Minneapolis is my home. My happiest memories are here. It's where I learned to ride a bike, had my first date, received my high school diploma. But today, I'm too afraid to even walk in my neighbourhood by myself.
The ACE Hardware down the street? The one that I used to bike to in the summer? Robbed twice in the past five days.

The Walgreens next to my elementary school? Molotov cocktail thrown into it.
The Lake Harriet Bandshell, where we spent countless Mother's Days? Homeless encampment popped up next door.
These are the things you don't read about in the news.

Ten minutes from my house, at 38th and Chicago, there is still an autonomous zone. Police are not allowed to enter. Residents have died because medical authorities couldn't get through, and carjackers (of which there are MANY) will speed into the zone to escape officer pursuit.

My favorite dinner theater canceled its production of Cinderella because it was "too white."

My church — my beloved, tiny, Lutheran church — organized social justice marches for our congregation while refusing to reinstate in-person services (they're still virtual, by the way).

And how about the week of the 2020 riots?

We lived under a curfew for days while looters seemingly roamed freely. Friends fled their home at 3:30 a.m. because the auto parts store behind them was on fire. And then we watched in horror as our City Council members demanded

that the city defund the police — as they hired armed security for themselves.
I no longer recognize Minneapolis. I no longer want to live here. We are done, and I am leaving.

I've spent the past year watching this city crumble. Burning it wasn't enough, I guess. Every day, I watched another piece of sanity and stability fall to the hysterical, bloodthirsty, self-righteous mob.
You distinguish between rioters and protestors? Racist. You do not want Marxist-inspired racial justice theories to be promoted in schools? Racist. You thought that maybe "Justice for George Floyd" should be left to the courts, and not mob rule? Super, super racist.
And where were our leaders providing stability and calm and confidence in the system? Nowhere to be found. What we did find were crazed politicians spouting fire and brimstone (I'm looking at you, Maxine Waters and John Thompson) and leaving us to pay the price.
Let me be clear: this city's demise wasn't just violent protests and burning buildings, or crime skyrocketing and businesses fleeing. It was also political indoctrination, hypocritical leadership, and the suppression of oppositional thought.
Any condemnation of the violence was denounced as "racist." Billboards stating simply "Support MN Police" were brutally vandalized. Schools supported BLM walkouts for their students, then shut down in-person classes for fear of violent riots.
And all of this happened against the backdrop of our illogical, inconsistent, overly oppressive COVID-19 restrictions.
It's easy to look at (for lack of a better word) disaster zones like these and mentally distance yourself from them. Yeah,

that's awful, but those people choose to live there. They're the ones electing these leaders. This is their problem.

Yeah, it is. It is our problem.
And I can't help but look around and wonder, "What happened here? Where exactly did it all go wrong?"
Was it the liberal mob? Identity politics? The cries of "RACIST!" when someone disagreed with a particular reaction or policy?
Was it conservative silence as the loudest voices got more and more radical?
Was it our acceptance that "we live in a blue area, this is just the way things are?"
How did it all happen so fast?

Whatever it was, I'm leaving this dark, surreal, twisted version of Minneapolis on Friday. And I pray to God that I never have to come back.   [End]

"To integrate with evil is to be destroyed with evil. What we want indeed, justice for us is to be set apart. We want, and must insist upon an area in this land that we can call our own, somewhere (where) we can hold our heads (up) with pride and dignity, without the continued harassments and indignities of our oppressors."

"The size of the territory can be judged according to our own population. If our people number one-seventh of Americas total population, then give us one-seventh of this land!"

"We must win our freedom from these blue-eyed devils by any means necessary!
    Malcolm X, Minister of the Nation of Islam,
        (The Black Muslims) 1964.

Published June 10, 2020

Economic pain worsens for Minneapolis as businesses exit after riots.

The city must focus on 'rebuilding right,' Chamber of Commerce says.

[Companies leaving Minneapolis after riots over the death of a Black man in police custody are compounding the array of economic challenges facing the city as it rebuilds and repairs, business leaders say.

Manufacturer 7-Sigma Inc., for instance, is departing after four decades, taking 50 jobs, a loss that Minneapolis can ill afford]

Economic pain worsens for Minneapolis as businesses exit after riots | Fox Business

Marc H. Morial, Contributor
President and CEO, National Urban League
50 Years Of Black Mayors
07/19/2017 05:06 pm ET Updated Jul 31, 2017

"To be an African-American mayor leading a city in the 21st century is not about "power" but about "possibilities." With more than 470 African-American mayors leading cities across the United States, the lens of our leadership is shaped from our own personal experiences. Together, we collectively bring a perspective that allows for a spectrum of possibilities." — Mayor Sylvester Turner, Houston, TX,

"The Role and Obligations of African-American Mayors in the 21st Century," State of Black America, May 2017

Fun Fact: The City of Washington DC could be BURNED to the Ground, TOMORROW, just as easily as Democrats/Blacks Supremist BURNED 500 square blocks of Washington DC, April 1968. So, the <u>Democratic Era of Government by Terrorism still hangs over America.</u>

As per the Civil Rights Movement, as per the Feminist Movement as per LILAC, etc etc. Straight, White, Male, Protestants are the Enemy of ALL other Americans. These people are a Weapon the liberals use to destroy, First World, White America and install its Dream of a Non-White, Third World America, a "Detroit from Sea to Shining Sea".

Note: The Black Ethnic Cleansing of Americas cities continues today as per Black Lives Matter, BLM, continued race war against White America.

[White Flight Today, White Flight Tomorrow, White Flight Forever?] by *Johnny Johnston, American Renaissance, December 5, 2020*

[Is there any alternative to economic collapse to get us to stop running?]

<u>White Flight Today, White Flight Tomorrow, White Flight Forever? - American Renaissance (amren.com)</u>

MALCOLM X THE BLACK REVOLUTION, JUNE 1963

"Actually, Americas most dangerous and threatening black man is the one who has been kept sealed up by the Northerner in the black ghettoes"   Malcolm X

"Since the black masses here in America are now in open revolt against the American system of segregation, will these same black masses turn toward integration or will they turn toward complete separation?
Will these awakened black masses demand integration into the white society that enslaved them or will they demand complete separation from that cruel white society that has enslaved them?
Will the exploited and oppressed black masses seek integration with their white exploiters and white oppressors or will these awakened black masses truly revolt and separate themselves completely from this wicked race that has enslaved us?"
"Not even in the Bible is there such a crime! God in His wrath struck down with fire the perpetrators of lesser crimes!
One hundred million of us black people! Your grandparents! Mine! Murdered by this white man. To get fifteen million of us here to make us his slaves, on the way he murdered one hundred million! I wish it was possible for me to show you the sea bottom in those days— the black bodies, the blood, the bones broken by boots and clubs! The pregnant black women who were thrown overboard if they got too sick!
Thrown overboard to the sharks that had learned that following these slave ships was the way to grow fat!"
"Why, the white man's raping of the black race's women began right on those slave ships! The blue-eyed devil could not even wait until he got them here!
Why, brothers and sisters, civilized mankind has never known such an orgy of greed and lust and murder.   "
"We want no integration with this wicked race. We want complete separation from this race of devils. But we should not be expected to leave America and go back to our homeland empty-handed. After four hundred years of slave

labor, we have some back pay coming, a bill owed to us that must be collected."

"If this white government is afraid to let her twenty-two million ex-slaves go back to our country and to our own people, then America must set aside some separate territory here in the Western Hemisphere, where the two races can live apart from each other, since we certainly don't get along peacefully while we are here together."

"To integrate with evil is to be destroyed with evil. What we want indeed, justice for us is to be set apart. We want, and must insist upon an area in this land that we can call our own, somewhere (where) we can hold our heads (up) with pride and dignity, without the continued harassments and indignities of our oppressors."

"The size of the territory can be judged according to our own population. If our people number one-seventh of Americas total population, then give us one-seventh of this land!"

"We must win our freedom from these blue-eyed devils by any means necessary!   Malcolm X

Well I can't write a US History book on the Civil Rights Movement and not include some interesting aspects of Americas first 'B' President.
 obama.
The 'B' does not stand for Black.
It actually stands for Bastard.
How Far America has fallen!

President obama, the Bastard.
obamas father already had a wife in Kenya before he "married" obamas mother. Just check out, http://www.politico.com/news/stories/0411/53968.html But White People are just too nice (almost) to mention this about their president.
" In 1961, while he was an undergraduate student at the

University of Hawaii, the school's foreign student adviser called an immigration official and said Obama had recently married StanleyAnn Dunham - the president's mother - despite already having a wife in Kenya."

Obama's father forced out at Harvard
The university was concerned about his personal life and finances, records reveal.
POLITICO.COM
https://www.politico.com/story/2011/04/obamas-father-forced-out-at-harvard-053968

obamas, Hatred of the White race.

Yes, obama (black, Muslim born) did Murder (Qaddafi) Libya's Leader (CIA ordered NATO fighter jets to bomb his convoy) and did start and back the civil war in Libya, that has caused the deaths of tens of thousands and the Suffering of Millions, all to put Libya into Americas Pocket, right next to Iraq and (soon) Syria. BUT when obama ordered his CIA Minions to Murder Qaddafi, <u>he also had an another Motive,</u>

to Destroy 'White, Christian Europe', just as Qaddafi had warned.
IE; The black African INVASION of Europe!
Some words from the Murdered Man. Some words from the Grave. And obama's Inspiration!

Qaddafi warned: "Europe . . . could turn into Africa. There is a dangerous level of immigration from Africa into Europe, and we don't know what will happen. What will be the reaction of the white Christian Europeans to this mass of hungry, uneducated Africans? We don't know if Europe will remain an advanced and cohesive continent or if it will be destroyed by this barbarian invasion."

The B-2's last combat deployment was in March 2011 when three aircraft were used in Operation Odyssey Dawn over Libya. Currently, there are 20 B-2's in the US Air Force's inventory.

obama support for World Terrorism, AKA the CIA.
This is very Funny as it was obama and his CIA that Created, funded, trained and armed the IS, (Islamic State) years ago, to help fight Assad of Syria.

The IS (Islamic State) is a Surrogate US Military force.
IS as CIA Child
Defense Intelligence Agency: "Establish a Salafist Principality in Syria", Facilitate Rise of Islamic State "In Order to Isolate the Syrian Regime"
Declassified DIA document

While initial mainstream media reporting is focused on the White House's handling of the Benghazi consulate attack, a much "bigger picture" admission and confirmation is contained in one of the Defense Intelligence Agency documents circulated in 2012: that an 'Islamic State' is desired in Eastern Syria to effect the West's policies in the region.

Astoundingly, the newly declassified report states that for

"THE WEST, GULF COUNTRIES, AND TURKEY [WHICH] SUPPORT THE [SYRIAN] OPPOSITION... THERE IS THE POSSIBILITY OF ESTABLISHING A DECLARED OR UNDECLARED SALAFIST PRINCIPALITY IN EASTERN SYRIA (HASAKA AND DER ZOR), AND THIS IS EXACTLY WHAT THE SUPPORTING POWERS TO THE OPPOSITION WANT, IN ORDER TO ISOLATE THE SYRIAN REGIME...".

The DIA report, formerly classified "SECRET//NOFORN" and dated August 12, 2012, was circulated widely among various government agencies, including CENTCOM, the CIA, FBI, DHS, NGA, State Dept., and many others.

https://www.judicialwatch.org/wp-content/uploads/2015/05/Pg.-291-Pgs.-287-293-JW-v-DOD-and-State-14-812-DOD-Release-2015-04-10-final-version11.pdf

obamas CIA, has killed over 500,000 Syrian, Men, Women and Children.

From Wikipedia, the free encyclopaedia
Arming Syrian rebels
Main articles: CIA activities in Syria, Timber Sycamore, and American-led intervention in Syria

An Army of Glory **fighter launches a** BGM-71 TOW **anti-tank missile at a Syrian government position during the** 2017 Hama offensive**.**
Between 2013 and 2017, under the aegis of the covert CIA-directed operation Timber Sycamore **and the overt Department of Defence-led** Syrian Train and Equip Program**, the US trained and armed nearly 10,000 rebel fighters at a cost of $1 billion a year.**[34] **The CIA had been sending weapons to anti-government rebels in Syria since at least 2012.**[35] **Some of these weapons reportedly fell into hands of extremists, such as** al-Nusra Front **and** ISIL.[36][37] **Former CIA analyst and** Brookings Institution **fellow** Bruce Riedel **has stated that Saudi support for the program has given** Saudi Arabia **greater say over American policy in the Syrian Civil War.**[38]

Casualties of the Syrian civil war
From Wikipedia, the free encyclopedia

Source	Casualties	Time period
Syrian Centre for Policy Research	470,000 killed[14]	15 March 2011 – 11 February 2016
UN and Arab League Envoy to Syria	400,000 killed[2]	15 March 2011 – 23 April 2016
Syrian Observatory for Human Rights	494,438–606,000 killed[1]	15 March 2011 – 30 May 2021

The Washington Monument is shown in the upper center of this picture.

Personal NOTE: How long before this Monument, to a Black Slave Owner, is Destroyed as all the rest of those White Monuments have been destroyed?
OR, will it be re-name after a Black Hero like George Floyd? We will see.

Now some Words from the Fall of the Government of the United States of America, April 1968.

[NOTE: I use the US Congressional Records a lot in this Book, as it is harder for the Liberals to Delete/Rewrite its information than other so-called, Historical Sources as everyone is watching, all the time. AFC]

From Congressional Record: Vol. 114, April 8. Pg. 9183.
Rep. Edwards of Alabama;
"Mr. Speaker, as smoke was billowing over Washington as a result of the riots this past weekend, I sat in my office contemplating the future of this great Nation. Troops were on the streets outside my window. A machinegun was set up on the steps of the Capitol and my secretaries had been sent home early because of the possible assault on the Capitol."
"What are we coming to? Martin Luther King is dead and whoever shot him must be found and convicted. But in the mean time, a vacuum has been created in the civil rights movement and it looks like Stokely Carmichael is moving into that void. This is not a very encouraging sigh. So whatever we thought of Martin Luther King, the assassin's bullet only made matters worst."
"In this atmosphere of violence, riots, looting, and burning, charged with emotions, we are asked to legislated. People are saying that now we must pass the civil rights bill with its open housing provisions, the gun laws, completely rebuild our cities. And we are told that it must be done now ---- without proper debate. Just pass it and get the riots stopped. But what happens then? Where does it stop? Must we

pass a new law every time there is a riot?"
"Reasonable men are being stripped of all
reason in their zeal to offer a balm in exchange
for peace and quiet.
Maybe I am unreasonable, but I am not willing
to legislate with a gun at my head: I am not
wiling to yield to those who would take the law
into their own hands: I am not willing to admit
that a handful of scum can dictate the policies
of this Government and tell the Congress
which laws to pass and which laws not to pass. I get my
back up when I feel this kind of illegal pressure being
applied."

From Congressional Record, Vol. 114, Pg. 9751, April 11, 1968.
As Washington DC Burned.
Hon. John R. Rarick of Louisiana.
"Mr. Speaker, the burning of our nation's capital has destroyed an estimated 600 buildings at an estimated loss of $13 million.
While the destruction was wide-spread, the "soul brothers" passed over--the burned-out area, if combined is estimated at 500 square blocks, or would form an area 20 blocks by 25 blocks.
 This is Washington DC alone----a city that has not been burned by a military enemy since the British...."

From Congressional Record, Vol. 114, Pg. 9738, April 11, 1968.
As Washington DC Burned.
Hon. John R. Rarick of Louisiana.
"...In the avalanche of propaganda, hypocrisy and falsehood that followed the death of King, the President and national

figures together with the news media have undertaken to eulogize and commit to martyrdom Martin Luther King, who under the guise of non-violence caused violence wherever he went."

"What do those who indulge in this hypocrisy seek? Political favor, martial gain, or the enactment of the "open housing law", which will destroy our Rights of property, liberty and freedom?

We are indeed a sick nation.

We witness in our major cities looting, theft, burglary, arson, robbery, murder. All indeed a fitting tribute to an advocate of violence.

From the Congressional Record, Vol. 114, Pg. 9616, April 10, 1968.
As Washington DC Burned.
Congressman Selden from Alabama.

"It will be recalled that when the Civil Rights Act of 1964 was passed, it was said here on the floor of the house that the passage of that legislation would take the civil rights movement off the street. (IE; Surrendering to Terrorist demands, [AFC])

Today, however, the House is being asked to consider yet another civil rights bill in a National Capital that in recent days has been under a virtual state of siege by looters and burners.

The House is being asked---if not in effect ordered and directed by extraordinary parliamentary procedures---to pass another civil rights bill while troops guard the Capital and patrol the streets protecting the Capital Building itself.

I submit that no legislation should be considered under such conditions in a free and democratic society.

The spurious notion has been advanced in recent days that somehow property rights are separate from, and not as important as, other rights under our system. But the face is that the foundations of the American system rest on the concept of the individual's right to hold property. The bill we are considering today is one of the most serious infringements on that right ever to be put before the American Congress. This is not a civil rights bill. It is a totalitarian bill which would sacrifice individual freedoms on the altar of election-year expediency.

I therefore ask that the House reject this highhanded effort to stampede the U S Congress into unwise legislation under conditions of siege."

From Congressional Record, Vol. 114, Pg. 9613, April 10, 1968.
As Washington DC Burned.
Congressman Clark from Pennsylvania.
"An examination of the Congressional Record will clearly indicate that, unfortunately, my predictions of disaster have come true this past weekend."
"I ask how many have talked to the police officers and National Guardsmen and federal troops who braved the war on Washington? And that is exactly what it has been--a war on Washington.
   Total and utter destruction of Blacks of the city creating havoc and spreading fear through this city such as has never been before. And now we are being asked to forge our usual 'calm', deliberative, legislative process, in an atmosphere of fear."
"It is beyond my wildest imagination that within the past 72 hours the people of this Nation saw television and newspaper pictures of a tripod and machinegun right

outside these doors on the very steps of the Capital Building and we still refuse to face the fundamental issue of this moment..."

From the Congressional Record, Vol. 114, Pg. 9534, April 10, 1968.
As Washington DC Burned.
Congressman Tuck of Virginia.
"The horrendous situation which now exists is accentuated by what appears to be a complete and abject surrender of the executive and legislative departments of our government to these ruthless racists, looters, thieves and incendiaries whose real object is to pillage and plunder and also destroy the Government of the United States."

From Congressional Record; Vol. 114, Pg. 9530. April 10, 1968. Mr. Abbitt of Virginia: as Washington DC BURNED. "The Nation is faced with armed insurrection and nothing worthwhile is being done by the administration to suppress it—only containment. Here we are today being asked to pass more civil rights legislation to deprive our law-abiding citizens of their rights and privileges."

"Never before in a free society has it been contemplated that the Government had a right to tell free people that they cannot sell their homes to whomever they choose. A man's home is supposedly in a free land to be his castle and here we find that the leadership of our Nation is trying to strike down this concept and compel free men and women to give up the right to control their own property and dispose of it as they see fit."

""Disorder is rampant in the land--- arson, armed robbery, murder, and rioting in the streets. The Nation is faced with armed insurrection and nothing worthwhile is being done by the administration to suppress it—only containment. Here we are today being asked to pass more civil rights legislation to deprive our law-abiding citizens of their rights and privileges. It is shocking to me that we now find ourselves in such a situation. It is shotgun action calculated to intimidate enough of the Members because of the grief throughout our land over the recent killing of a prominent citizen and the armed insurrection on the other hand of a vast lawless element."

From the Congressional Record, Vol. 114, Pg. 9531, April 10, 1968.
As Blacks BURN 500 square blocks of Washington DC. Congressman Burleson of Texas.
"I think if I were for this so-called Civil Rights bill, with it's open housing feature, I would not want to cast my vote for it, while soldiers and marines are having to stand guard in front of this Capital. I resent threats of force and duress in

anything and if I had to legislate under such conditions I would walk out of this Chamber and not return. "

"It is a sad commentary on this Congress if it yields to the pressures of the moment. I for one had rather yield my seat in this House than to do so."

From the Congressional Record, Vol. 114, Pg. 9531, April 10, 1968.
As Washington DC Burned.
Congressman Hungate from Missouri.

"Mr. Speaker, we meet in the midst of 13,000 troops called to protect life and property against the threat of imminent destruction. Three blocks from this Chamber shops and stores are boarded up against further pillaging. Three blocks from the White House buildings are looted and burned. This may be the way to move this Congress. It is not the way to move this Congressman. "

From the Congressional Record, Vol. 114, Pg. 9405, April 9, 1968.
As Washington DC Burned.
Congressman John R. Rarick of Louisiana.

"Mr. Speaker, I can sell my home or rent my apartment to anyone I want to---right now.

So can any American. At this time any American can refuse to sell or rent to anyone if he pleases not to.

But should the misnamed Fair Housing Act--become law none of us could sell or rent to anyone we desire."

"Likewise, shameful is the use of smears to blame riots on the poor man. To the contrary, reports from the battle of Washington, show the majority of the looters seized have jobs----in fact a sizable number are Federal employees."

From the Congressional Record, Vol. 114, Pg. 9368, April 9, 1968.
As Washington DC Burned.
Congressman John R. Rarick of Louisiana.

"But....as a matter of cold, hard fact, this nation---the land of the free----is moving relentlessly toward such a fate....as government by law gradually submits to the Blackmailers on America."

"Our government of laws, our government of constitutional processes, has begun to crumble before a tide of lawlessness which has not only been condoned but even encouraged by many government leaders."

"The watts riots in California served as Lesson No. 1 in large-scale Blackmail. This outbreak of mass crime was not punished. It was rewarded with countless millions of federal dollars poured into the area in the hopes that the rioters would "cool it".

After the demonstration of largess, can you blame the Negroes of Detroit, Newark, Milwaukee, Chicago, and scores of other American cities for wanting to get into the action?"

" It's widely said that the government is motivated by a desire to placate the troublemakers.

Actually the reverse situation prevails. The trouble makers are Blackmailing our government.....successfully and repeatedly. They seek money....and power. They're getting both."

From the US Congressional Record, Vol. 114 ;
Rep Dowdy (D-Texas) As DC Burned; April 1968:

"Let us not forget that the police power has broken down under racial attack in the past few days....do we really want to create this situation in the suburbs? We are being asked to forget the Constitution, to destroy the private property system on which our nation has been built, and to further endanger the life and limb of our citizenry, young and old, to grant special privileges to a 10% minority group."
From Congressional Record: As Washington DC Burned, April 1968.
Rep. Sikes of Florida.
"I look around me in the Nation's Capital City with a sad and heavy heart. All of us are shocked by the fury of the violence which engulfed our Nation last week. We deplore murder and destruction at any level."
Yet I see arising from the tragic events of last week not an acceptance of responsibility in government and among the people but a demand for new programs and more benefits. It is time, Mr. Speaker to say there must be no profit from riots. It is time for our Nation to hear about the acceptance of responsibility. That is what our country needs most.

Hundreds of millions of dollars have been poured into programs to improve the lots of the people. The inhabitants of Washington live better than those of any other capital city in the world. They have greater advantages and more opportunities. Yet the headlines were filled last week with occurrences here and elsewhere which repudiate every principle for which America stands.
 The great efforts and the huge expenditures that have been made have been rewarded by burning and stealing and mob violence. And if it had not been stopped by force, the mob would have burned down the Capital City of the Untied States and very probably it's Capital buildings."
"Yes, this is a sad day for all of us but not a day for those of us here in the House to be shocked into a surrender of our

responsibilities as legislators. It is a day for the Congress to face up to the truth about what is going on. What happened here would not have been tolerated anywhere else in the world.

The rioters were not carrying on the work of Martin Luther King or venerating the principles credited to him. They were out to loot and destroy and appeals to reason by their President or their leaders had no effect. It was the stern application of force in the face of lawlessness. And nothing else, that was respected. I hope this important lesson is not lost on the Nation Today."

From Congressional Record, Vol. 114, Pg. 9185, April 8, 1968.
Mr. Rarick of Louisiana, as Washington DC burned.

"What kind of a leader have the American people in the White House?

The Nation's Capital has been burned and sacked: the criminal element given freedom to trample the rights of all law-abiding citizens: and what did the President (LBJ) do? He met with provokers of the revolution and proclaimed again." We shall overcome." "Overcome what?"

Does anyone recall the President of the United States taking to television and appealing for law and order using his entrusted position to calm the passions of primitive peoples and opportunists? Why the 20-hour delay before calling troops into the District?

Do we have a President of all people or a commander in chief of the revolution in the White House?"

By RICHARD REEVES, Special to The New York Times. New York Times (1857-Current file). New York, N.Y.: Apr 10, 1968. pg. 1, 2 pgs

From Congressional Record Mr. O'Hara of Michigan: As Blacks rioted, Looted and BURNED 500 square blocks of Washington DC, 1968.

"The Johnson administration is threatening your Representative with a complete cut-off of Federal contracts in your district if he does not vote "yea" "But these threats are nothing compared with the active campaign of intimidation, terror and Blackmail being waged by Black power and civil-rights militants who plan to burn down the districts of those voting "nay." Some Members of Congress have even been threatened with physical violence against their persons and families."

Note; Any 'law' passed under 'Duress', IE; the 'Threat of Violence' is illegal and unenforceable.

From Congressional Record:
Mr. Byrd of West Virginia;

"… what happen over the weekend in Washington and in other cities was entirely unjustified and, in my judgment., had no logical connection whatsoever with Dr. King's death. As I viewed the looting and other lawlessness, as shown on television, it was evident that a carnival and festive spirit was prevailing, as children and adults, with their arms filled with loot, with garbage cans filled with loot, with grocery carts filled with loot, passed before television cameras, smiling and waving their hands to the TV viewers."
"Men and women carried away refrigerators, living room furniture, bedroom furniture, wearing apparel, whisky, and everything they could get their hands on, in an atmosphere of levity. It was a shameful and disgraceful performance before the Nation and the world, as thousands of people took advantage of the opportunity to go on a rampage."
"I will also hope that Federal troops will remain in this city indefinitely, because if Washington is to be subjected to a

summer campaign of demonstrations, as has long been planned, the presence of Federal troops will be reassuring."

Day 8, Friday April 12th, 1968. WASHINGTON—
In a Capitol still anxious over rioting only a few blocks away and still protected by roving patrols of helmeted marines, the House of Representatives last week completed Congressional action on a far-reaching civil rights bill that will pull down racial barriers in 80% of the housing market. "The Fair Housing Act of 1968".

JFK's Civil Rights Address, June 11, 1963 Lyrics

https://genius.com/John-f-kennedy-civil-rights-address-june-11-1963-annotated

Good evening, my fellow citizens:

This afternoon, following a series of threats and defiant statements, the presence of Alabama National Guardsmen was required on the University of Alabama to carry out the final and unequivocal order of the United States District Court of the Northern District of Alabama. That order called for the admission of two clearly qualified young Alabama residents who happened to have been born Negro. That they were admitted peacefully on the campus is due in good measure to the conduct of the students of the University of Alabama, who met their responsibilities in a constructive way.

I hope that every American, regardless of where he lives, will stop and examine his conscience about this and other related incidents. This Nation was founded by men of many nations and backgrounds. It was founded on the principle that all men are created equal, and that the rights of every man are diminished when the rights of one man are threatened.

Today, we are committed to a worldwide struggle to promote and protect the rights of all who wish to be free. And when Americans are sent to Vietnam or West Berlin, we do not ask for whites only. It ought to be possible, therefore, for American students of any color to attend any public institution they select without having to be backed up by troops. It ought to to be possible for American consumers of any color to receive equal service in places of public accommodation, such as hotels and restaurants and theaters and retail stores, without being forced to resort to demonstrations in the street, and it ought to be possible for American citizens of any color to register and to vote in a free election without interference or fear of reprisal. It ought to to be possible, in short, for every American to enjoy the privileges of being American without regard to his race or his color. In short, every American ought to have the right to be treated as he would wish to be treated, as one would wish his children to be treated. But this is not the case.

The Negro baby born in America today, regardless of the section of the State in which he is born, has about one-half as much chance of completing a high school as a white baby born in the same place on the same day, one-third as much chance of completing college, one-third as much chance of becoming a professional man, twice as much chance of becoming unemployed, about one-seventh as much chance of earning $10,000 a year, a life expectancy which is 7 years shorter, and the prospects of earning only half as much.

This is not a sectional issue. Difficulties over segregation and discrimination exist in every city, in every State of the Union, producing in many cities a rising tide of discontent that threatens the public safety. Nor is this a partisan issue. In a time of domestic crisis men of good will and generosity should be able to unite regardless of party or politics. This is not even a legal or legislative issue alone. It is better to settle these matters in the courts than on the streets, and new laws are needed at every level, but law alone cannot make men see right. We are confronted primarily with a moral issue. It is as old as the Scriptures and is as clear as the American Constitution.

The heart of the question is whether all Americans are to be afforded equal rights and equal opportunities, whether we are going to treat our fellow Americans as we want to be treated. If an American, because his skin is dark, cannot eat lunch in a restaurant open to the public, if he cannot send his children to the best public school available, if he cannot vote for the public officials who will represent him, if, in short, he cannot enjoy the full and free life which all of us want, then who among us would be content to have the color of his skin changed and stand in his place? Who among us would then be content with the counsels of patience and delay?

One hundred years of delay have passed since President Lincoln freed the slaves, yet their heirs, their grandsons, are not fully free. They are not yet freed from the bonds of injustice. They are not yet freed from social and economic oppression. And this Nation, for all its hopes and all its boasts, will not be fully free until all its citizens are free.

We preach freedom around the world, and we mean it, and we cherish our freedom here at home, but are we to say to the world, and much more importantly, to each other that this is the land of the free except for the Negroes; that we have no second-class citizens except Negroes; that we have no class or caste system, no ghettoes, no master race except with respect to Negroes?

Now the time has come for this Nation to fulfill its promise. The events in Birmingham and elsewhere have so increased the cries for equality that no city or State or legislative body can prudently choose to ignore them. The fires of frustration and discord are burning in every city, North and South, where legal remedies are not at hand. Redress is sought in the streets, in demonstrations, parades, and protests which create tensions and threaten violence and threaten lives.

We face, therefore, a moral crisis as a country and a people. It cannot be met by repressive police action. It cannot be left to increased demonstrations in the streets. It cannot be quieted by token moves or talk. It is a time to act in the Congress, in your State and local legislative body and, above all, in all of our daily lives. It is not enough to pin the blame on others, to say this a problem of one section of the country or another, or deplore the facts that we face. **A great change is at hand, and our task, our obligation, is to make that revolution, that change, peaceful and constructive for all.** Those who do nothing are inviting shame, as well as violence. Those who act boldly are recognizing right, as well as reality.

Next week I shall ask the Congress of the United States to act, to make a commitment it has not fully made in this century to the proposition that race has no place in American life or law. The Federal judiciary has upheld that proposition in a series of forthright cases. The Executive Branch has adopted that proposition in the conduct of its affairs, including the employment of Federal personnel, the use of Federal facilities, and the sale of federally financed housing. But there are other necessary measures which only the Congress can provide, and they must be provided at this session. The old code of equity law under which we live commands for every wrong a remedy, but in too many communities, in too many parts of the country, wrongs are inflicted on Negro citizens and there are no remedies at law. Unless the Congress acts, their only remedy is the street.

I am, therefore, asking the Congress to enact legislation giving all Americans the right to be served in facilities which are open to the public -- hotels, restaurants, theaters, retail stores, and similar establishments. This seems to me to be an elementary right. Its denial is an arbitrary indignity that no American in 1963 should have to endure, but many do.

I have recently met with scores of business leaders urging them to take voluntary action to end this discrimination, and I have been encouraged by their response, and in the last two weeks over 75 cities have seen progress made in desegregating these kinds of facilities. But many are unwilling to act alone, and for this reason, nationwide legislation is needed if we are to move this problem from the streets to the courts.

I'm also asking the Congress to authorize the Federal Government to participate more fully in lawsuits designed to end segregation in public education. We have succeeded in persuading many districts to desegregate voluntarily. Dozens have admitted Negroes without violence. Today, a Negro is attending a State-supported institution in every one of our 50 States, but the pace is very slow.

Too many Negro children entering segregated grade schools at the time of the Supreme Court's decision nine years ago will enter segregated high schools this fall, having suffered a loss which can never be restored. The lack of an adequate education denies the Negro a chance to get a decent job.

The orderly implementation of the Supreme Court decision, therefore, cannot be left solely to those who may not have the economic resources to carry the legal action or who may be subject to harassment.

Other features will be also requested, including greater protection for the right to vote. But legislation, I repeat, cannot solve this problem alone. It must be solved in the homes of every American in every community across our country. In this respect I wanna pay tribute to those citizens North and South who've been working in their communities to make life better for all. They are acting not out of sense of legal duty but out of a sense of human decency. Like our soldiers and sailors in all parts of the world they are meeting freedom's challenge on the firing line, and I salute them for their honor and their courage.

My fellow Americans, this is a problem which faces us all -- in every city of the North as well as the South. Today, there are Negroes unemployed, two or three times as many compared to whites, inadequate education, moving into the large cities, unable to find work, young people particularly out of work without hope, denied equal rights, denied the opportunity to eat at a restaurant or a lunch counter or go to a movie theater, denied the right to a decent education, denied almost today the right to attend a State university even though qualified. It seems to me that these are matters which concern us all, not merely Presidents or Congressmen or Governors, but every citizen of the United States.

This is one country. It has become one country because all of us and all the people who came here had an equal chance to develop their talents. We cannot say to ten percent of the population that you can't have that right; that your children cannot have the chance to develop whatever talents they have; that the only way that they are going to get their rights is to go in the street and demonstrate. I think we owe them and we owe ourselves a better country than that.

Therefore, I'm asking for your help in making it easier for us to move ahead and to provide the kind of equality of treatment which we would want ourselves; to give a chance for every child to be educated to the limit of his talents.

As I've said before, not every child has an equal talent or an equal ability or equal motivation, but they should have the equal right to develop their talent and their ability and their motivation, to make something of themselves.

We have a right to expect that the Negro community will be responsible, will uphold the law, but they have a right to expect that the law will be fair, that the Constitution will be color blind, as Justice Harlan said at the turn of the century.

This is what we're talking about and this is a matter which concerns this country and what it stands for, and in meeting it I ask the support of all our citizens.

Thank you very much. JFK

"Who controls the past controls the future. Who controls the present controls the past." George Orwell

Full (Government Deleted) News story.
  SOUTH BEND TRIBUNE
December 16, 2000
N. D. Sociologist accesses information on race riots from archives
Research Pipeline By KEN BRADFORD
Tribune Staff Writer
kbradford@sbtinfo.com
(219) 235-6257
© Copyright 2000 South Bend Tribune. All rights reserved.
Record Number: MERLIN_2094552

Dan Myers is amazed at his good fortune. Information is the crude oil of academic research.

It provides the fuel for new ideas and knocks the rust off the old ones.

And Myers, a sociology professor at the University of Notre Dame, is sitting on a geyser of material that had been whispered about among researchers in his field. Myers, almost by accident, controls the archives from the Lemberg Center for the Study of Violence, formerly at Brandeis University.

He and his students are working their way through the archives, which detail thousands of race riots that occurred between 1966 and 1973.

"Previously, research said there were a couple hundred race riots during that period." he said. "We haven't been through everything here yet, but we already know of at least 3,500 incidents."

"There are hundreds and hundreds of riots most people didn't even know about. This will give us a fuller picture of what was going on," he said.

Race riots were part of the volatile fabric of the mid-'60s. Anyone old enough to watch TV at the time will recall footage on the national news of stores ablaze and the bloody faces of rioters and police officers alike.

A riot that began Aug. 11, 1965, in the south central Los Angeles neighborhood of Watts resulted in 34 dead, 1,000 injured and 4,000 arrested.

Two major riots followed in 1967. A three-day free-for-all in Newark, N.J., in mid-July resulted in 26 dead, 1,100 injured and 1,600 under arrest. Two weeks later, in Detroit, a riot left a death toll of 43.

For Myers, 34, riots carry no personal interest. He was born in Xenia, Ohio, after the Watts riot and was still in diapers during the Newark and Detroit riots.

He started looking into race disturbances as an undergraduate at Ohio State University. His interest grew, and he was working on his doctorate at the University of Wisconsin when he heard murmurs of a vast collection of documents on race riots.

He made inquiries but was unable to find this legendary archive.

But after he moved to Notre Dame in 1977, he received a phone call that unraveled the mystery. The answer was to be found at Manchester College in North Manchester, Ind. Brandeis, a Jewish-sponsored school just outside of Boston, had received gift money that allowed it to open the Lemberg Center for the Study of Violence. From 1966 to 1973, the center compiled newspaper clippings, taped interviews and paid for a Roper Poll study about race riots.

By 1973, racial violence was becoming less common, and the Lemberg Center closed.

A story in The Justice, the Brandeis student newspaper, from Sept. 18, 1973, attributed the closing to a decrease in funding and a sense that the center had completed its task. There also was concern in the Brandeis community that information gathered at Lemberg would be used to help (white) mayors "put down riots and further oppress city (Black) populations," The Justice reported.

(Yes, it would seem the Lemberg archive was 'lost' intentionally. AFC)

In any case, the center closed and the archive suddenly had no home. "For a time, all this was stuffed under a stairwell at Brandeis," Myers said.

Eliot Wilczek, archives assistant at Brandeis, said there was no formal university archive then. He said the decision to transfer the materials on permanent loan to Manchester College, affiliated with the Church of the Brethren, was made in 1979.

Ferne Baldwin, the longtime archivist at Manchester, said the college probably seemed like the logical place for the materials.

"Negro snipers turned 140 square blocks north of West Grand Blvd. into a bloody battlefield for three hours last night, temporarily routing police and national guardsmen.... Tanks thundered through the streets and heavy machine guns clattered....

The scene was incredible. It was as though the Viet Cong had infiltrated the riot-Blackened streets."

Excerpted from *The 1967 Detroit Rebellion*, *Revolutionary Worker #915, July 13, 1997*

"They came here primarily because we had the first peace studies major in America." she said. "It was quite a large collection, and it was here a long time."

But it was a little-known resource, used only by a handful of researchers." "When Notre Dame expressed an interest, we were quite willing to let them have it," Baldwin said.

One of Myers' sources told him about the Manchester collection. "When I called and asked about it, the person who answered the phone said she could see it from where she was sitting," he said.

When he rushed down to see it, he wasn't disappointed. He's worked out an agreement involving Brandeis, Manchester and Notre Dame that leaves the archives under his care.

It's been quite a task sorting and organizing the materials. Thousands of yellowing newspaper clippings from papers all over the country now are arranged in file cabinets in a Flanner Hall office. Each clip provides nuggets of information about an event that could be researched.

Lemberg staff members also recorded extensive interviews in 10 American cities– on reel-to-reel tapes as well as cassettes– that need to be examined.

The center also paid the Roper polling organization to interview 6,000 Americans about race relations and civil unrest.

"It's a really great data set," Myers said. "No one's really analyzed it all yet."

To pull together all this information nowadays would require visits to hundreds of newspaper offices and other sites. The beauty of an archive is that all this information now is in one place, Myers said. Tony Perez, a senior from St. John, Ind., has based two projects, including his senior thesis, on the archives.

In one, he's comparing how riots in smaller cities were covered by larger newspapers and smaller newspapers. To his surprise, the larger papers, which would be more remote, seemed to have provided more background and context for the violence. Smaller papers seemed to concentrated more on what happened than why it happened.

The archive was essential. "Without this, I'd be chasing bits and pieces everywhere," he said "The Lemberg archive was the backbone.

Matt Baggetta, a senior from Johnstown, N.Y., used the old interview transcripts from community leaders to explore people's opinions of the rioters.

"People needed to explain what they were seeing," Baggetta said. "It mostly came down to two ways of looking at it."

"Some thought rioters were just people caught up in the heat of the moment. Others believed rioters were trying to make a statement through a very extreme means of protest."

Without the Lemberg archive, he wouldn't have done the study, which has been submitted to the Sociological Quarterly. "I never would have come up with the idea without this unique data set," he said.

He has 16 students, most of them seniors, working on projects related to the materials. Some are in his Riots and Protest class, and others are in a special studies group he leads.

Myers said benefits from the Lemberg archive should go beyond academic use to public policy applications.

For example, a good argument could be made that poor training and tactics may have made riots of the 1960s even worse.

"There was an attitude that you could bust people back into line," he said. "Police were so insistent on arresting people just for spitting on them."

The current trend, which research might support, is for police to back off from angry confrontations instead of helping them escalate, Myers said. "Police seem to be a lot smarter about controlling crowds."

There are dozens of other directions the research can go- from riots in schools, to bias in media coverage, to efforts at introducing calmer voices during periods of unrest.

And two questions Myers hears often have yet to be answered.

"People ask all the time whether we're going to have riots again," he said.

Without doing all the research, he suspects there are great similarities between then and now, with the gap between the rich and poor growing even larger. But that's just one of the factors.

Another question is whether the violence actually accomplished anything.

Myers said interviews conducted through Lemberg seemed to be asking that same question. It will be useful to measure the responses then against what people would say now."
[End]

Daniel J. Myers, Ph.D.
president@misericordia.edu

Personal note: This Lemberg Archive News article was removed from the Net shortly after I used it as a source in an article. It has also been removed from the archives of the South Bend Tribune itself. Thus 'here' is the last place you will see this information.

I am told that my Books should 'help' the people that read them be better people and to be able to live better, safer, lives, so here goes.

Here is the 'Solution' for White people living in today's America.
That it is the verysame 'Solution' as it was for millions of White South Africans when South Africa fell to Black Rule, is obvious. AFC

Story in the Business Insider;
Wealthy Americans are racing to get the EU's last remaining 'golden passport' before it's gone.
Hannah Towey
Fri, February 17, 2023

For the first time, Americans are applying for golden passports and visas more than any other nationality, according to Henley & Partners' 2023 USA Wealth Report**, released Thursday.**

Retiring Overseas | Get Results | resultsdistributor.com
https://resultsdistributor.com/retiring overseas/now

How to leave the U.S. and retire abroad - CNBC
https://www.cnbc.com/2020/09/14/heres-how-to-leave...

Top 10 Countries to retire abroad for Americans | GCS
https://www.globalcitizensolutions.com/top-10...

How to Retire Abroad: 12 Tips for Retirement Overseas
https://www.newretirement.com/retirement/how-to...

The Best Affordable Places to Retire Overseas in 2021 ...
https://money.usnews.com/money/retirement/

EPILOGUE

"With this book I have tried to give you a small taste of what Americas BURNING was like. Outside of OPEN WAR, it is Humanly impossible to comprehend the destruction, the TERROR, of over 5,000 Race Riots, 250,000 Riot FIRES.

That America has buried these events 'out of time' and teach lies to their young, might keep the Cities from burning, or not, but it is still a lie.

Is America a lie?

But as I said, with 78% of Americans today enjoying the PRIVILIGES, the POWER, the MONEY, the JOBS, from all that TERROR, well who could, would dare, complain."   AFC

If you have any Comments or Questions, you can contact me, (No Profanity please) at, adriancerny@yahoo.com

Personal NOTE:

A First World America, is/was, a "White Mans" Creation.
Just as Freedom was/is a White Man's Creation.
BUT, ALL the World and ALL of America, HATED White men, thus the WAR that brought Down White Men, along with White Man's Freedom.
Along with White Man's First World America!
Welcome to the Third World, America!
"Forever" as there is no one, now, to lift you back up. AFC

Fighters from the Failed Cause for a Free, First World, America.

Americas Future. A rich, beautiful Past turned into Marxist ruins. (Detroit)

BETRAYED

America's Conquest of the White Man

by A.F. CERNY

The Mongrel Historian

Printed in the USA
CPSIA information can be obtained
at www.ICGtesting.com
LVHW010424210224
772321LV00016B/769